The BRIC Road to Growth

PERSPECTIVES

Series editor: Diane Coyle

The BRIC Road to Growth

Jim O'Neill

LONDON PUBLISHING PARTNERSHIP

Published by London Publishing Partnership
www.londonpublishingpartnership.co.uk

ISBN: 978-1-907994-13-5 (pbk.)

A catalogue record for this book is
available from the British Library

This book has been composed in Candara

Copy-edited and typeset by
T&T Productions Ltd, London

Cover design: Kate Prentice

Contents

Preface

At the time of going to press, it is highly fashionable to write off the emerging markets story of the past decade or so. Not only is this a mistake, but most people in the West have no idea how far the centre of economic gravity has already shifted away from the United States and Europe, and how quickly this shift occurred. This profound change in the global economy is not something that might happen at some point in the future; it is already the reality. Since 2010, for example, the increase in the US dollar value of GDP for the eight largest emerging economies has been more than $3.5 trillion, close to the equivalent of creating a new Germany.

The fact of this shift away from a Western-dominated global economy to one with other, stronger, engines of growth has some important consequences. This book focuses on two: the lessons for the West from the success of alternative models of growth, and the urgent need for changes in global economic governance arrangements.

The 'adaptive' capitalism practised by the Growth Market countries, especially China and South Korea, has lessons for the Western European and North American economies as they struggle with the legacy of the 2008 financial crisis and underlying structural problems. We in the West need to learn from the world's fast-growing economies, just as much as they need to learn from us. Of course, they have to adapt their own models further, but equally so do we. These economies have apparently succeeded in positioning their financial institutions to serve the prevalent needs of their nations, with less focus on a goal of short-term profit performance. Their success in supporting and encouraging so many of their people to devote a significant amount of their time to gaining a better education and to adapting new technologies suggests other areas we can perhaps learn something from.

The BRIC economies (Brazil, Russia, India and China) have been adding the equivalent of a new Italy to their combined GDP each year; China itself has been adding another Spain annually, while the contribution to world growth from the BRICs and other emerging countries in the past decade exceeds that of all of Europe and the United States put together. Even if China's growth rate remains slower this decade than it was in the 2000s, it will still attain a pace of economic growth never achieved by the United States over a ten-year period. The first cities running on battery-operated cars will be Chinese, not American. Some of the near future's most important scientific innovations and new technologies will come from South Korea, not Britain or Germany.

This is already the reality. When the euro was launched, Germany expected that France would always be its biggest trading partner, but, going on current trends, by 2020 Germany will be exporting twice as much to China as to its euro-zone neighbour.

The second issue concerns the institutions of global economic governance, which urgently need to change to reflect today's realities. Many policymakers, especially in the West, are in denial over the facts of the current global economy. While many talk excitedly about exporting to emerging nations, most are unwilling to give up any of their dominance of international institutions to give these countries representation to match their growing importance. Although the increasing influence of China and the other BRIC countries and Growth Market economies is appreciated, it is often seen as something that could have an impact at some point in the future, not as having in fact happened some time before the 2008 'North Atlantic crisis' (as many in Asia describe it). The sooner the global shift is understood, the sooner a new and more effective set of institutions for global governance can come about. The BRIC countries must have a place in key institutions, including the IMF and the World Bank. Europeans need to step back and be prepared to learn from today's fast-growing emerging economies.

The rate of growth the BRIC countries have been enjoying will slow. Such a rapid pace cannot continue indefinitely, and, moreover, the fast-growing economies need to give a higher priority to the quality of growth and the needs of their citizens. The fast-growing emerging economies face a range of economic, social and political challenges. The unrest in Brazil and Turkey is a warning signal about the importance of both governance and quality-of-life issues. However, the likely slowdown compared with the 1980s to 2000s should not become an excuse for dismissing the BRIC phenomenon as hype. Their growth performance will continue to outstrip the economies of the West, with their profound structural problems.

For our part, we in the West must be less dogmatic than in the past in assuming our model of capitalism is best. China and the other BRIC countries can offer important lessons to the rest of us, about the role of the state and of local culture, even though they all have significant economic and political challenges ahead of them. We *all* need to embrace the era of adaptive or flexible capitalism. And we will *all* benefit from international organizations and governance that reflect the present reality of the global economy, not its distant past.

Chapter 1

What's been happening in the BRIC countries?

It is nearly twelve years since I first coined the acronym BRIC to highlight the remarkable impact these rapidly growing countries were starting to have on the rest of the world, as well as the changes they were experiencing for themselves. The first decade of that period, as I have described elsewhere,[1] turned out to be even more dramatic than I had anticipated, but as we move further into the second decade, there is evidence of slower economic growth in each of Brazil, Russia, India and China. Some observers are now suggesting that the tailing off of BRIC growth means that the whole phenomenon was overhyped[2] and was never a great investment proposition anyway.[3] It is true that the BRIC economies are currently growing by less than in the past decade, but it is not clear whether this is a structural slowdown or just a cyclical one. For reasons I outline below, it was highly unlikely that they would have continued to see GDP growth at the same rapid pace.

Moreover, while it is interesting to look at their collective economic performance, it is also clear that there are big differences between the four economies. China is of particular importance, as the next chapter will discuss in more detail.

Table 1.1. BRIC real GDP growth by decade.

	1981–90	1991–2000	2001–10	2011	2012	2011–20
China	9.3	10.5	10.5	9.3	7.8	7.5
India	5.6	5.6	7.5	6.3	3.9	7.5
Brazil	1.6	2.6	3.6	2.7	0.9	5.2
Russia	–	−2.1	4.9	4.3	3.6	5.4
BRICs	5.3	5.5	8.1	7.7	5.8	6.6

Source: IMF and Goldman Sachs Asset Management (GSAM).

Table 1.1 shows GDP growth for each of the BRIC countries by decade, going back to the 1980s, along with my 2010 forecast for the ten years to 2020, and actual growth rates in 2011 and 2012. The figures tell the story of a decade of unusually strong growth, followed by a return to a less astounding, but hardly disappointing, growth performance. It is clear that the decade 2001–10 was a particularly good one for the BRIC economies. In some ways, it may have been unusually fortunate, maybe even a 'perfect storm' for rapid growth. In particular, nothing went badly wrong in any of the four countries, which was spectacularly lucky given their diversity in terms of their economies, societies and vulnerabilities to external influences. This is one of the main reasons (as I explained in *The Growth Map*[1]) that real GDP growth during that decade far exceeded expectations.

Perhaps to the casual observer a further acceleration in growth after the 2000s might have seemed inevitable. To those of us with experience in these economies, and in studying long-term growth trajectories in general, it seemed highly likely that the growth of the BRIC economies would slow down. The Goldman Sachs (GS) forecast for this decade was 6.6% on average, which would seem to be a more sensible benchmark than the extremely rapid growth of the previous decade. Anything lower would count as disappointing. If growth now starts to slow either to less than this figure, or even to less than the previous thirty years together, the adjective 'overhyped' would be justifiable. (As it turns out, average BRIC real GDP growth for the three decades 1981–2010 was also exactly 6.6%.)

As can be seen, primarily because of China's importance, BRIC growth in 2011–12 has been 6.7%. Although slightly higher than the past thirty-year average, it is, of course, well down from 2001–10. At the time of writing, consensus forecasts for 2013 and 2014 are 6.6% and 6.9%, respectively. So while the BRICs' real GDP growth this decade might be disappointing compared with the surge of 2001–10, it has actually slightly surpassed my initial expectations.

The detail obscures an extremely important point. Even with slower GDP growth in the next ten years compared with the previous decade, the impact of the BRIC economies on the world is still increasing. Figure 1.1 makes this point, which is vastly underappreciated by so many people, powerfully.

By the end of 2011, the aggregate size of the BRIC economies stood at around $15 trillion, not far off the size of the US economy. Remarkably, in just one year (2011) the rise in the dollar value of their GDP was $2.3 trillion, equivalent to creating between seven and eight new Greek economies a year, or to adding another Italy to the global economy in a year. In the West, people think about the BRIC countries as economic powers of the future. The point is that this future is already upon us. They are the powers of the present.

The message of this book is that even though their growth rates may be slowing down, Western policymakers must take

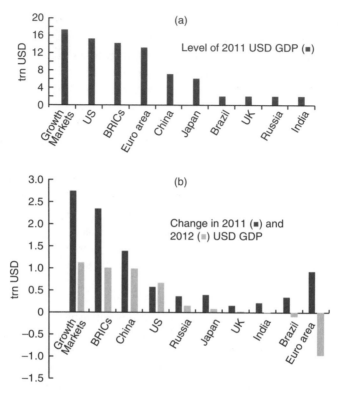

Figure 1.1. (a) The size of key economies in 2011.
(b) Change in USD GDP. *Source*: IMF.

on board the lessons of the adaptive capitalism adopted in a wide range of economies, from China to Nigeria, and must allow these Growth Markets their proper status in international institutions, for effective governance of the global economy.

The BRIC countries differ greatly from the other Growth Markets, but the common theme is that they have been pragmatic in adapting capitalism to their own situation and needs. This book describes some of the key similarities and differences between them. They need to become more Western in some of their own policies and practices, as described below. However, the West, post crisis, needs to adapt too.

I have spent much of the past eighteen months trying to explain to business people and investors around the world that, hard as it might be for them to believe, the European financial crisis is not the biggest issue facing the world economy. The biggest single issue is the continuing growth of the BRIC countries, and some other rapidly growing economies. As I will discuss in a geopolitical and policy context, they will soon outweigh the United States in terms of GDP, which, among other things, will mean that as a group their influence on the world is set to rise dramatically.

Labelling economies

In the past few years the label BRIC has, for political rather than economic reasons, become BRICS with the inclusion of South Africa. Economically this is a bit odd, as South Africa, with a total GDP of around $400 billion, is not much bigger than Greece. Its size is dwarfed by the four original BRIC countries, and, indeed, by the four other emerging economies[4] that I refer to here as Growth Markets (Mexico, Indonesia, South Korea and Turkey). They are each two or three times the size of South Africa. While the BRICs and the Growth Markets are the main subject here, as I will show in Chapter 3, Africa as a whole is already showing promising signs of growth and its potential is certainly quite BRIC-like. What is more, the growth of trade and investment between Africa and the BRIC countries is an important aspect of the transition into a mainly non-Western world economy – a story that is currently underappreciated. Nigeria is the continent's leading contender for growth economy status. Still, if South Africa can help to both represent Africa as

Table 1.2. Global growth: last three decades and next decade.

	1981–90	1991–2000	2001–10	2011–20 (forecast)
US	3.3	3.4	1.6	2.5
UK	2.8	2.5	1.4	1.5
Euro area	2.4	2.3	1.2	1.5
Japan	4.6	1.2	0.7	1.0
China	9.3	10.5	10.5	7.5
India	5.6	5.6	7.5	7.5
Brazil	1.6	2.6	3.6	5.2
Russia	–	–2.1	4.9	5.4
BRICs	5.3	5.5	8.1	6.6
Growth Markets	5.1	5.2	6.9	6.2
World	3.3	3.3	3.5	4.2

Source: IMF and GSAM.

a continent and use that platform to positively encourage the growth of infrastructure and trade between African countries, then its membership of the club is more justifiable.

Still driving global growth

Table 1.2 is probably the most important table in the book because it shows that, although BRIC growth is going to be slower this decade than last, global GDP growth this decade could accelerate compared with the past three decades, because the BRIC countries and other rapidly growing emerging world economies now have so much more weight in the global economy.

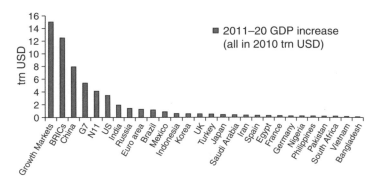

Figure 1.2. Contribution to GDP (USD) 2011–20.
Source: GS Global ECS Research.

By 2015 the size of the BRIC economies in US dollar terms will surpass that of the United States. This means that if their growth rate exceeds that of the United States, their contribution (in current US dollar terms) to world GDP growth will be more than double that of the United States as can be seen in Figure 1.2. In purchasing power parity (PPP) terms, or, in other words, with GDP adjusted for the cost of living in different countries, the relative size of the BRIC countries is even larger. This is the basis on which global GDP growth rates are normally calculated and compared, but some people argue that PPP calculations distort the contribution of the BRIC countries. Even on the nominal US dollar basis, though, their 6.6% growth contribution is more than double that of the United States. Another way of thinking about it is to imagine what world GDP would look like if the United States grew by 6.6%. Seen in this light, one could even argue that it is a good thing that the BRICs' real GDP growth will slow as their economies get bigger, as otherwise there would be even more dramatic changes in world trade.

As I discussed in *The Growth Map*,[1] long-term growth is really driven by two variables: the number of people in a country's

Table 1.3. Labour force participation.

	Size of working age population (millions)	Growth this decade of working age population
China	1,013	0%
India	822	16%
Euro area	219	−2%
US	213	4%
Brazil	137	11%
Russia	102	−8%
Japan	79	−9%
UK	41	1%

Source: UN and GSAM.

workforce and how productive they are. Countries with large and rising numbers in the workforce, and with rising productivity, will see their real GDP growth rates accelerate, and countries with declining populations, and weak and declining productivity, will see their growth rates weaken. Table 1.3 sets out the conflicting pressures for each of the BRIC countries.

As things stand, none of the BRIC countries has the 'ideal' combination. India easily has the best demographic profile; its large, young population gives it a rapidly increasing labour force and the highest potential growth rate of all the BRIC economies. I frequently think that, for this reason alone, India has the highest potential to do better than expected in this decade and beyond. In contrast to this, India probably has the weakest productivity of the four BRIC countries. As explained elsewhere,[1] I use an index produced by GS and based on a total of eighteen different variables, called a growth environment score (GES), to measure sustainable potential growth and productivity. India scores the lowest of the BRIC

Table 1.4. Trend growth in the BRIC countries (% change in real GDP).

	Realized			2050 projections by decade*			
	1981–90	1991–2000	2001–10	2011–20	2021–30	2031–40	2041–50
Brazil	1.6	2.6	3.6	5.2	4.6	3.9	3.1
Russia	–	–2.1	4.9	5.4	3.8	2.7	1.8
India	5.6	5.6	7.5	6.5	6.0	5.6	5.1
China	9.3	10.5	10.5	7.1	5.2	3.4	2.9

Source: IMF and GS Global ECS Research.
*From GS Global ECS projections model.

countries and has the most need – but also the most scope – to improve. If it did introduce the reforms needed to boost productivity, it surely has the greatest capacity to achieve unexpectedly strong growth. India could easily surprise us, despite its disappointing progress in the past two years.

In June 2013, I visited India to meet the probable candidate for the BJP (Bharatiya Janata Party) in the 2014 elections, Mr Modi, the chief minister of the state of Gujarat. If he were to become elected, despite considerable challenges, and if he could implement his mantra of 'maximum governance and minimum government', India could become an extremely exciting place. Poor governance, both centrally and in many regions, has hindered the effectiveness of many policies, economic ones included. Transformation of central governance and its links to the different states would be a huge, but very difficult, step forward for India.

None of the other three countries has as favourable a demographic profile as India, and so, in order to boost real GDP growth significantly, they have to rely more on productivity-enhancing policies to exceed expectations. So it is difficult to believe that their growth will accelerate in the future. Brazil has reasonable demographics and, with much improved policies that could unleash private sector investment, it could also show stronger growth than over the last decade. I have assumed that Brazil will grow by more, and this currently looks somewhat optimistic.

Once economies become very big, of course, there is less scope for them to grow rapidly. So, by 2050, it is assumed that all four of the BRIC countries will have slowed down. The two with the most challenging demographics are China and Russia, which both have ageing populations. Yet in the decade 2040–50, the BRIC countries combined will have surpassed the G7 in size, having overtaken the United States some twenty years earlier. Their average growth rate of 3–4% over that period, while significantly slower than today's 6–7%, would still be the envy of Europe and the United States.

While all four of the BRIC countries need to introduce policies to boost their productivity, there is a danger of being too pessimistic about their outlook. There is evidence that demographic trends in Russia and China will not be as bad as I have just assumed. In March 2012, I participated in the annual workshop of the Ambrosetti Forum and, in a session on the 'emerging world', the chief economist of Sberbank compared official Russian projections for population size in recent years and the latest estimates of the actual figures. It would seem that the population has increased slightly, and so, as yet, shows little evidence of the widely assumed decline. There continues to be growing evidence that, as Russians become wealthier and more knowledgeable, they are adopting behavioural attributes that are extending their life expectancy. This includes drinking less cheap alcohol, especially vodka. There are perhaps other factors at work as well, including some signs of increased immigration from some of the countries of the former Soviet Union.

Russia faces considerable challenges, but so far this decade its growth has been slower than previously, but not materially slower than I expected.

It is worth underlining once again the significant position the BRIC countries already hold in the world economy: if Russia grows, as assumed, by 5% on average this decade, its contribution to global GDP will be bigger in US dollar terms than that of the euro area.

What about China's demography, the result of its all-too-successful one-child policy? Recently, the State Council announced the closure of a number of ministries, including the one responsible for overseeing this policy. Some people see this as another sign that the one-child policy is in the process of being relaxed. If so, and if China's birth rate were to rise as a result, this would not affect China's labour force until well after 2020, but by 2030 China's population would not be shrinking to the degree currently assumed.

Turning from workforce size to productivity, each of Brazil, Russia and India need to introduce policies to boost their performance. Suppose that they decided to learn from the experience of South Korea. At the end of 2012 South Korea had the second highest GES of the 180 countries in the ranking, and it is also the only large populated emerging nation that has approached the living standards of the G7. Policymakers in each of the BRIC countries, and many of the so-called Next 11 (N11)[6], might find it useful to study South Korea and see what they can learn for their own economies.

South Korea's potential would be spectacular if it were as large as one of the BRIC countries, but its population of less than 50 million is tiny by comparison. However, if Korea were to ever unify so that the North harnessed the forces that have driven South Korea, the potential of the unified nation would be ultimately rather strong, despite the enormous adjustment challenges.

What could the other BRIC countries learn from South Korea's productivity advances? The lessons fall into three different categories.

Firstly, South Korea scores well in terms of education. To varying degrees, each of the BRIC countries could follow suit, India especially. It could be argued that repeating South Korea's success in education for populations the size of those of the BRIC countries is a much tougher challenge, but, according to the Organisation for Economic Co-operation and Development (OECD), Shanghai has probably the best secondary education standards in the world today.[7] So it is not an impossible challenge.

Secondly, South Korea has achieved superb results in the introduction and adoption of modern technologies such as mobile telephones and computers and in its broadband Internet access and use. South Korea actually scores the best of any of the 180 countries in the rankings on this front. The remarkable progress of Samsung in global markets is a vivid example of this technological prowess: it is a leading-edge technology company. Technological know-how benefits all sectors of Korean society, in both visible and less visible ways. Each of the BRIC countries, to varying degrees, could benefit dramatically from the nationwide spread of modern technologies. India has the greatest need to change, and would get the greatest potential benefit from catching up.

The third area relates to the rule of law, especially with regard to business. South Korea is not up to the highest of those standards achieved by some developed economies, but it has improved considerably since the 1997–98 Asian crisis, and the vulnerabilities that revealed. The propriety of connections between business and government and a credibly enforced rule of law are vitally important for sustained growth. The alternative – cronyism, uncertainty about the regulatory and legal environment, and even the risk of expropriation of assets – means lower investment and slower growth.

All the BRIC countries, especially India, could benefit from better governance. Their growth performance will be inhibited if they do not address some important domestic governance shortcomings. Even with such changes, their growth will not be as spectacular as it has been in the recent past. But, for at least the rest of this decade, they will be driving world growth.

The long-predicted shift in global economic power has now happened; in the West, we have not yet made the necessary mental adjustment and continue to talk about this as a transition that still lies ahead. Yet the BRIC countries and other fast-growing emerging economies account for about 30% of world GDP and for about 70% of all world growth in GDP since 2000. This means that we will need to look to the BRIC countries and other emerging Growth Markets for economic dynamism, and I will turn to that future in later chapters. First, though, it is important to understand the absolutely key role China has played in transforming the economic map of the world.

Chapter 2

The Chinese century

The previous chapter highlighted the astonishing degree of change in the world economy. It is essential to understand that China is at the heart of this story. As noted in Chapter 1, in 2011 the GDP of the BRIC economies increased by $2.3 trillion, adding the equivalent of another Italy to the world economy. Of this increase, nearly $1.4 trillion was due to China's growth. David Cameron seems to have understood the implication; at the Conservative Party Conference in October 2012, he pointed out that the previous year China had created the economic equivalent of another Greece every thirteen weeks. However, many people seemed unaware of the relative importance of China's growth; everywhere I travelled (including China) during 2011 and 2012, the only subject people wanted to discuss was Greece. I developed a stock answer: that it is a lovely country but, in the context of the world economy, just not very important.

The Chinese themselves do not always appreciate their relative importance in the global economy. They often still see themselves as merely an emerging economy with many impoverished people and little global relevance. As recently as July 2013, on a brief trip to Beijing, I gave a presentation to an audience of over 300 distinguished business people long involved in Sino–British trade, the 'Icebreakers' of the 48 Group Club, and even there, based on the reactions to my comments, they had little awareness of their huge impact on the world.

To drive home the point, consider that, at the end of 2012, China's nominal GDP had increased to $8.2 trillion, another $900 billion increase compared with the end of 2011. That followed a $1.4 trillion increase the previous year. Even within the BRIC context, these figures are remarkable. Understandably, people often compare China and India, not least because they are the only nations with more than a billion people. But China's GDP is now more than three times the size of India's, and China's growth is currently creating another India (or indeed another Russia) every two years. China is now the same size as the other three BRIC economies put together, and even though China's growth rate is slowing, it is still contributing a lot more to world GDP growth than the other BRIC countries.

Two further statistics demonstrate China's remarkable scale, and the scale of the mental adjustment we need to make to grasp this essential feature of the global economic landscape. First, the 7.5% real GDP growth I am predicting for China this decade, although slower than its growth rate in the previous three decades, is the equivalent of 4% annual real growth in the American economy. To find a similar performance in the United States you have to go back many years to when it was a far smaller economy. Second, this 7.5% growth means that China will contribute as much to world nominal GDP as the United States and the eurozone put together. This is utterly transforming world trade and the balance of economic power on a scale not widely appreciated.

A new China?

If China's economic growth does attain that figure of 7.5% on average during the decade 2011–20, then (depending on the value of its currency against the US dollar) the size of the Chinese economy will be nearly the same as that of the US economy. Goldman Sachs has been predicting that China will overtake the United States in nominal terms by 2027. Not only do many of us struggle to comprehend the speed and scale of China's ascent so far, but the fact that China's growth is decelerating compared with the previous thirty years is further complicating the story. Some observers have suggested that this slowdown may be the beginning of the end of the China story. But in doing so they fail to recognize that one of the main reasons China is slowing is because the authorities there believe that a better quality of growth is necessary now, and that the medium-term sustainability of growth will be enhanced by slowing down from past rates of expansion.

Why has China decided that 'less is more'? There are a number of important structural reasons, and also one shorter-term cyclical reason. Following the 2008 global credit crisis, which at its most severe in late 2008 threatened the collapse of the financing of world trade, Beijing unleashed a huge monetary and fiscal expansion to offset the slowdown in Chinese exports and to stimulate growth. The expansionary policies were oriented towards boosting infrastructure investment. Where necessary, direct state-backed investment was stepped up. The policy worked all too well because by late 2009 real GDP growth was already surprisingly strong, and it quickly became apparent that such aggressive counter-cyclical policies were increasing inflationary pressures and exacerbating some deep-seated structural problems in the economy. For example, as early as September 2009 Chinese policymakers were worried about a property market bubble developing, and they began to introduce a series of steps aimed at limiting excessive speculative purchases in China's cities. Beyond the specific challenges of the property market, policymakers also grew understandably worried about signs of an unwelcome surge in inflation. The dramatic escalation of the European economic and financial crisis dominated the attention of Western analysts and policymakers in 2010. But in China, where the financial crisis is known as the 'North Atlantic crisis', getting inflation back down to 3–4% from 6–7% was the main policy priority. Higher inflation is even more damaging than normal in a society like China's, where so many urban migrants aspire to increase their wealth and, therefore, save a high proportion of their income.

This development in the wake of the financial crisis encouraged China's leaders to think more carefully about its many long-term challenges, particularly the structure of the society and its governance. What is the point of 10% annual growth if the winners are a privileged few, and the losers fall further and further behind? The tremendous increase in inequality undermines the very core premise of modern Communist Party thinking, and has become something of a threat to social order. If economic growth is destabilizing Chinese social stability, is it worth it? Other symptoms of pressures arising from this rapid growth were price rises in food and other natural resources, and continued environmental degradation. These had become paramount policy concerns by 2010.

The post-crisis challenges join some well-known longer-term issues facing China. Of these, the main one is the demographic challenge, summed up in the saying that the Chinese 'will get old before they will get rich'. This is partly a result of the success of the one-child policy. To offset a declining workforce, the only way to sustain real GDP growth is to boost productivity. This is exactly why Chinese policymakers have come to regard the quality of growth as more important than the quantity.

Soon after the November 2012 to March 2013 leadership change, the authorities announced measures to reduce the number of separate entities for Chinese state policy – including abolishing the body that had been solely responsible for presiding over the one-child policy. To some observers, this hints that the one-child policy will soon be abandoned, given the worry about the demographic challenge. This area of policy will be the most important to watch, but it is unlikely to be the only big change in the 'new China'.

Chinese policy priorities and goals

The twelfth Five-Year Plan, published in spring 2011, set out China's policy priorities with some clarity.

The first is to double the size of the Chinese economy, and the wealth of Chinese citizens, by 2020. A real GDP growth rate of 7.5% (the same figure that I am predicting for the decade) is needed to deliver this goal. While actual GDP growth has regularly exceeded the official assumptions in the past, many forecasters disregarded official projections of growth. In the foreseeable future, this would not be wise. If real GDP growth turned out to be 9–10% or higher, it would probably be discouraged.

Secondly, the Chinese leadership appears to be more determined that growth is more equally shared and that the increase in income inequality be put into reverse. One of the easiest and most likely ways of pursuing this is a deliberate policy to boost wage growth among the lowest income groups, and it is part of the strategy to focus on increased consumption.

Whether this is sufficient remains doubtful, and other initiatives such as full citizen 'rights', including property ownership for migrant workers, access to health care and pensions, are probably necessary as well. Estimates of China's Gini coefficient (a standard measure of income inequality) show that progress in reducing inequality has been minimal, probably adding to pressure for new policies to achieve these goals. I have suggested that they abandon the phrase 'migrant workers' completely if a central part of their plan is to boost both their ability and willingness to consume. I pursued this notion in Beijing, discussing the idea privately with a number of business people and with some senior policymakers. They responded almost universally that to embrace such a radical idea quickly across all of urban China could be disruptive and, without permanent jobs being available, possibly costly, so it was not practical. But it was clear to me, listening to the policymakers, that this is something they are in the process of doing for real in the 'smaller' cities, and will continue to implement over the next couple of years. This is gratifying, because to empower these people is to help them enjoy the same benefits as many other urban dwellers, and it will give greater credence to the notion that a 'new' China is in train.

Thirdly, in the past couple of years Chinese policymakers have spoken with increasing frequency about the importance of knowledge and innovation, often linked to specific industrial strategies for more advanced and modern industries. Making a transition from low-value manufacturing and assembly to high-value innovative production is a priority. How this can be achieved in a society where individuals still have some of their personal choices restricted is of course a major question, but it is very interesting to see how often these policy priorities are mentioned by the senior leaders. Many of them are happy to discuss the issues. Not all share the same views, with some believing that it is just an attractive phrase that will not be followed by any specific actions. Others, including some in policymaking positions, said, quite specifically, that enhancing intellectual property rights and the legal system for business more generally would allow their rapidly rising university-educated population to pursue more creative business paths. One such policy advisor told me they have very little choice, as there are 6 million people graduating each year from China's universities, all of them very capable and skilled in the use of modern technologies.

Fourthly, and closely linked to the other goals, boosting consumption as a share of GDP is a priority. Along with this, there is a stated goal of a lower balance of payments current account surplus. This will be good news for the rest of the world, for if China consumes more, relative to what it produces, it will allow export growth elsewhere, and will reduce the tensions that occur in international trade due to China's mammoth export surplus. Each month when China releases its regular economic statistics, I look at a quick indicator of progress on this front: the relative performance of retail sales compared with industrial production (IP). Figure 2.1 suggests that China is heading in the right direction, albeit erratically.

This is critical for a better balance of world growth. The United States needs to produce more and consume less, while China needs to produce less and consume more. The United States needs to run lower current balance of payments deficits and China needs to run lower current account surpluses. Judging by the evidence so far, we can take some comfort from the fact that each is heading in the right direction. As Figures 2.2 and 2.3 show, the US current account deficit is now around 3% of GDP compared with above 6% before the crisis, and China's surplus has dropped sharply to around 2.5–3% of GDP from above 10% before the crisis.

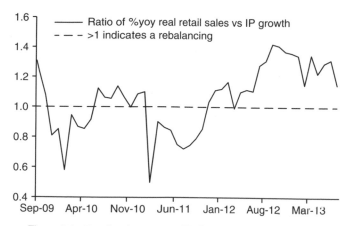

Figure 2.1. Retail sales versus IP. *Source*: CNBS and GSAM.

From the Chinese perspective, achieving a lower current account surplus through higher consumer spending and increased imports will also reflect a better balance of savings and investment within China. It is easy to conclude from this need for a better balance that Chinese people do not consume much at all, but that is incorrect. While it is true that the share of consumption in GDP declined significantly during 2001–10, the absolute value of consumer spending increased sharply. Indeed, the reported increase over the decade of around $1.6 trillion was equivalent to that of all the other BRIC countries combined. Even assuming that the share of consumption in GDP in China has not increased since 2010, this equates to a nominal increase of $800 billion in consumer spending in just two years. In all likelihood, the increase will have been closer to $1 trillion.

Looking forward to the remainder of the current decade, if China's nominal GDP were to increase by around $1 trillion per year (so at a slower pace than in 2011–12), this would take nominal GDP to $16.3 trillion by 2020, and, on conservative

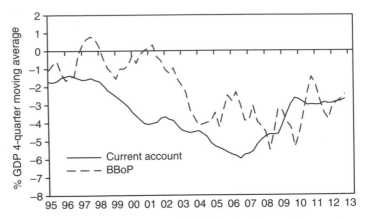

Figure 2.2. US current account deficit. Broad balance of payments (BBoP) = Current account + Net FDI + Net portfolio investment. *Source*: BEA.

assumptions, the increase in consumer spending would be $3.2 trillion. This would be close to the equivalent of another German economy in eight years. So for the rest of us, in both the developed and emerging worlds, whether or not China can succeed with its policies to support increased consumer spending is an important question.

Higher wage growth for the lower paid is a credible policy to try and ensure that consumer spending rises and inequality starts to be addressed. On the other hand, if these wage increases undermine China's international competitiveness, then there will have to be corresponding forces that ensure that the domestic savings rate continues to fall. This will require thoughtful policies to encourage Chinese companies to hoard less cash and distribute more of their retained earnings. It is important that the personal savings rate is also encouraged to decline, which will require that Chinese income earners have greater confidence in the health and security of their own and their families' futures, as many Chinese people save

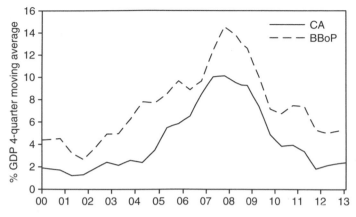

Figure 2.3. China's current account surplus.
Source: CNBS, SAFE and GSAM.

large amounts for precautionary purposes. Although less explicit in the twelfth Five-Year Plan, and in the usual leadership speeches, as discussed earlier, the government is continuing to pursue policies to give more rights to migrant workers, so that they too can consider home ownership and have access to medical care and social benefits, including some sort of pension. Without developments like these, Chinese consumption will not be capable of increasing in the way we might all hope. As mentioned earlier, why not get rid of the definition of migrant workers itself if they are serious?

In a somewhat sobering analysis of the policy challenges, Xia Bin,[8] a well-regarded academic, published in March 2013 a list of what needs to change in China. On his list, two additional goals were identified as critical: further substantial reform of the financial markets and the guarantee of secure property rights for rural land owners. Xia Bin calls for an accelerated plan for financial reform, allowing for the market determination of both interest rates and the exchange rate, to not only encourage much greater participation in the financial markets but also more competition and better choices for Chinese borrowers and savers. Deeper markets in some areas of finance might reduce the repeated emergence of asset price bubbles. For example, the soaring price of urban property appears to reflect in part the lack of alternative investment outlets for rich Chinese individuals. Articles such as the one by Xia Bin set out serious challenges, but in general they make me optimistic that, as in so many other areas, Chinese policymakers know the economic challenges they face and do not shy away from them.

It therefore seems likely that at some point improved land ownership rights will be introduced. This would clearly be a big confidence boost for rural families and also help increase their levels of consumption.

The other stated policy priorities are very closely intertwined, namely, a strong commitment to improve energy efficiency and to develop usable alternative energies. Given the commitment that China has made to double personal incomes, and to grow the share of consumer spending in the economy, many people wonder how genuine the policy commitment to energy efficiency and energy alternatives is. At an event in London in late 2012, where I was chairing a discussion about the policy priorities of the new leadership, I asked the Chinese ambassador to the United Kingdom the following: 'Which is more important to China, to increase the share of consumption in GDP or to improve energy efficiency?' The ambassador said it was both, and added that the Chinese leadership was quite used to handling complex challenges. I frequently find myself considering whether perhaps China's form of government and society gives the country a greater chance of success in meeting such complex challenges. For example, compared with the United Kingdom, it seems much easier to direct official financial support to financing alternative forms of energy. It would not be surprising if China were the first country in the world to have some cities running completely on battery-operated cars.

If energy efficiency and alternative energies are policy priorities numbers five and six, a seventh and final priority on the list is social harmony. This is not a new goal in China, but what is new and interesting is that, when articulated by policymakers, it is no longer first but rather last on the list. Nevertheless, Western observers should always remember that this striving for social harmony reflects a genuine and deep belief. This core belief in social harmony explains *why* we are looking at a 'new' China, valuing the quality of growth as more important for its 1.3 billion people than the sheer quantity of it. It is significant that social harmony is last on the list, behind factors like the importance of knowledge and innovation, and it is worth pondering the meaning of this. But in the spirit of the ambassador's answer, China is capable of handling complex goals and adapting the market economy to its own culture and needs. Or at least, we should all hope so.

Chapter 3

Beyond BRIC

China and the other BRIC countries are important in the global context, but they are being joined by a number of other large economies as the main drivers of world economic growth. In *The Growth Map*[1] I discussed the idea of the 'Next 11' (N11) emerging economies, after the BRIC countries. Exciting as their prospects are, the conclusion was that none of the N11 countries has the potential to be as big as any of the BRIC countries. Some that might approach Brazil or Russia in size include Indonesia, Mexico, South Korea, Turkey and possibly Nigeria, and certainly, if it could act collectively as a continent, Africa. Various acronyms have been coined for subsets of this group, MIST or MINT, removing South Korea and replacing it with Nigeria. Of these countries, the most significant is South Korea.

The South Korean model

The more time I spend in finance and economics, the more I find myself thinking that South Korea is unique, and could offer a model for many other nations, emerging and developed alike. In 2012, South Korea rose to second place out of 180 countries in the Goldman Sachs growth environment

Table 3.1. Growth environment scores.

	South Korea	China	Brazil	Mexico	Russia	Turkey	Indonesia	India	US
Headline	7.9	5.5	5.4	5.1	5.3	5.2	4.8	3.9	6.8
Corruption	5.9	3.7	5.4	4.3	2.8	5.2	3.6	3.9	7.5
Rule of law	7.0	4.1	5.0	4.1	3.4	5.2	3.7	4.8	8.2
Political stability	5.5	3.6	4.9	3.6	3.3	3.2	3.4	2.6	6.1
Openness	5.2	3.6	1.8	3.8	2.5	2.9	3.0	3.3	2.1
Investment	5.7	9.1	3.9	4.1	4.6	4.0	6.5	5.9	3.0
Government deficit	6.2	4.4	3.7	3.3	5.8	4.9	4.2	0.7	0.2
Public debt	8.1	8.6	6.4	7.6	9.3	7.8	8.6	6.3	4.3
Inflation	10.0	9.6	9.3	10.0	8.8	9.3	9.6	8.7	10.0
Life expectancy	9.2	7.7	7.6	8.3	6.8	7.7	6.8	6.0	8.7
Schooling	9.6	6.5	8.0	6.8	7.3	7.1	6.4	4.7	8.8
Personal computers	7.5	0.7	2.1	1.9	1.7	0.8	0.3	0.4	10.0
Mobile subscriptions	10.0	6.4	10.0	8.1	10.0	8.5	8.8	6.1	9.0
Internet users	9.3	3.9	4.6	3.5	4.9	4.5	1.2	0.9	8.4
Internet servers	9.9	0.0	0.2	0.1	0.1	0.6	0.0	0.0	6.2
Patent applications	10.0	2.0	0.8	0.9	2.0	0.3	0.1	0.2	10.0
R&D	8.0	3.7	3.0	0.9	2.6	2.1	0.2	2.0	7.1
Cost of starting a business	8.5	9.7	9.5	8.9	9.8	8.9	8.2	5.3	9.9
Urbanization	9.2	5.6	9.4	8.7	8.2	7.9	5.6	3.5	9.2

Source: GS Global ECS Research.

score (GES) rankings. This is remarkable; not only is it considerably higher than the other Growth Market countries, it is also above the United States.

The scores in Table 3.1 are an index of sustainable growth and productivity, with 10 being the best possible and 0 the worst.*

On some components, especially the technology indicators, South Korea attains the highest score. When policymakers from many other N11 countries ask for advice, I often tell them to get on a plane to Seoul and figure out what they can learn from South Korea and adapt to their own societies. I would give the same advice to Western policymakers. South Korea scores extremely well on education, and its improvements over time for the whole of its population should encourage many developing country leaders in the realization that it is possible to improve education for large numbers of children in our societies. The second striking area of South Korean success is technology. For many emerging economies, especially those with large and remote rural areas and undeveloped physical infrastructure, encouraging and supporting the use of new technologies can allow their societies to leapfrog intermediate stages of infrastructure development. There are clear signs of this occurring in Nigeria, for example, in both agriculture and banking.

The fact that South Korea scores so highly is not just an intellectual curiosity, because there is a close correlation between the GESs and wealth. In this regard, South Korea's

---

*The GESs are an average of six separate groups of variables, all of which are perceived to be relevant to productivity, with each group including a number of variables. It total, there are eighteen, and they are adjusted to have a score of 0 to 10. They are then aggregated for a single score. GS Global Paper 217 summarizes the concept in more detail.

progress in terms of incomes and broader indicators of human development should be a striking example to many aspiring developing economies. The Human Development Report of the United Nations Development Programme (UNDP) for 2012, *The Rise of the South*, shows that South Korea leads a group of around forty countries of the 'South' that have made stronger progress on the human development index (HDI) since 1990 than might have been expected.[9] Figure 3.1 shows the remarkable rise of South Korean GDP per capita, a reasonable proxy for a country's wealth, since 1960.

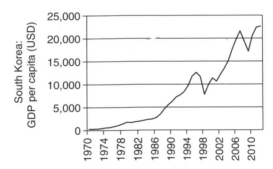

Figure 3.1. Wealth since 1970. *Source*: BoK.

A unified Korea?

In a fascinating article in the *Financial Times*, early in 2013, a journalist from the Chinese Central Party School newspaper argued that China should stop supporting North Korea's current policies and should consider encouraging it to seek unification with the South. Within two weeks of this article appearing, a UN vote to tighten sanctions over North Korea was not blocked by China, which added to my belief (or hope) that a new approach may be afoot from North Korea's only ally in the international community. While it is too early to jump to conclusions, perhaps this is the beginning of something significant, and the idea of a peaceful unification of the two Koreas is not entirely unrealistic.

As described in the previous chapter, long-term economic growth depends on the number of people who work and on their productivity. South Korea, like many other countries, does not have a good demographic profile. It resembles Japan in its ageing population, but with a time lag. On the other hand, South Korea has a dramatically less developed neighbour to the north of some 25 million people who could provide a demographic boost if unification were possible. German unification is a vivid demonstration of the challenges involved, but also an important source of lessons about what mistakes to avoid.

From BRIC to MINT

Figure 3.2 shows which countries could be defined as Growth Markets by 2050.

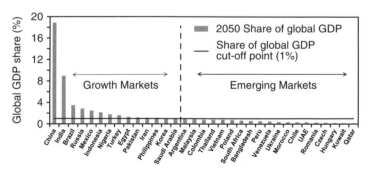

Figure 3.2. Growth Market economies by 2050.
Source: GS Global ECS Research and GSAM.

Table 3.2. GESs for the MINT countries.

		Mexico	Indonesia	Nigeria	Turkey
	Headline	5.1	4.8	3.7	5.2
Political conditions	Corruption	4.3	3.6	2.7	5.2
	Rule of law	4.1	3.7	2.5	5.2
	Political stability	3.6	3.4	1.1	3.2
Macro-economic conditions	Openness	3.8	3.0	4.1	2.9
	Investment	4.1	6.5	—	4.0
Macro-economic stability	Govt deficit	3.3	4.2	5.5	4.9
	Public debt	7.6	8.6	9.0	7.8
	Inflation	10.0	9.6	8.1	9.3
Human capital	Life expectancy	8.3	6.8	3.3	7.7
	Schooling	6.8	6.4	3.2	7.1
Technology	Personal computers	1.9	0.3	0.1	0.8
	Mobile subscriptions	8.1	8.8	5.5	8.5
	Internet users	3.5	1.2	2.7	4.5
	Internet servers	0.1	0.0	0.0	0.6
Micro-economic environment	Patent applications	0.9	0.1	—	0.3
	R&D	0.9	0.2	0.6	2.1
	Cost of starting a business	8.9	8.2	2.9	8.9
	Urbanization	8.7	5.6	5.5	7.9

Source: GS Global ECS Research.

China will continue to tower over all the others, accounting for nearly 20% of world GDP, with India a somewhat distant second with around 10% of world GDP, then Brazil and Russia, each with less than 5% of world GDP. Of the N11, the four largest will indeed be the MINT countries. While none of the four will reach the size of a BRIC economy, collectively Mexico, Indonesia, Nigeria and Turkey could account for around 10% of world GDP, close to the size of the euro area. While there is no natural economic affinity between the four countries, as they grow there is exciting potential for them, and for other countries with closer historical or geographical links to them.

Mexico

More than any of the other N11 countries, Mexico could have the biggest gripe about not being included as a 'BRIC' back in 2001. It is not too far behind any of those countries in terms of the size of its GDP, and its demographics are quite favourable. That said, Mexico's economy achieved a significantly disappointing performance from 2001–10, and this was despite the huge increase in crude oil prices, which should have helped Mexico as much as it helped the other big oil producers.

In terms of its GES, Mexico lies behind Turkey but ahead of Indonesia and Nigeria. It is also behind Brazil, China and Russia. Mexico's score is helped by the rather strong performance of some of its key macroeconomic indicators, such as its relatively low and stable inflation rate and its reasonably sound public finances. Indeed, its cyclically adjusted fiscal balance and debt position would be envied by many developed economies, and it would easily satisfy tough criteria for sound public finances. These macroeconomic foundations are also shared by both Indonesia and Turkey, as Table 3.3 shows. This explains why each of these countries is becoming so popular with global fixed income investors. Mexico's debt-to-GDP ratio of just 40% and its cyclically adjusted deficit of 2% would put virtually any major developed economy to shame.

Table 3.3. Cyclically adjusted budget balance and debt/GDP for MINT countries.

	Cyclically adjusted budget deficit (%GDP)	Gross general government debt (% GDP)
Brazil	−2.7	67.2
India	−8.8	66.4
Mexico	−3.7	43.5
Turkey	−1.6	35.5
Korea	2.3	32.5
Indonesia	−1.4	23.6
China	−0.9	21.3
Russia	0.5	10.4

Source: ECB.

By early 2013, Mexico had become one of the most popular destinations for investors, a far cry from previous times, with its sound fiscal position being at the core of this new-found optimism. But there are a growing number of reasons for optimism about its economic prospects.

Unlike many larger emerging economies, including nearby Brazil, Mexico appears to be highly competitive in terms of labour costs. While it is not straightforward to compare countries, Mexico stands out on most international measures. This position has been helped by the considerable shift in China's competitive position due to its wage increases in recent years. Being so close to the 300 million consumers in the US market appears to be helping Mexico as China shifts to its new priority of domestic and consumer-led growth. Auto production in Mexico in particular appears to be very strong.[10]

On top of this rising competitiveness, business is also attracted by the efforts at major reform introduced by the current president, Enrique Peña Nieto, with the focus on reforming the bloated oil sector and the inefficient state-controlled Pemex. At a time when it has become fashionable for other large emerging nations to strengthen state control of their energy companies (such as Petrobas in Brazil or Gazprom in Russia), this shift in the opposite direction on Pemex is eye-catching.

Efforts to dramatically reduce the impact of the violent drug cartels that have tarnished Mexico's image so much in recent years are another central feature of the reforms. Presumably, if solid economic growth can be maintained and incomes rise, it will have a positive impact on these efforts.

According to the last Goldman Sachs projections for 2050, Mexico is likely to be the fifth largest of those countries still regarded as 'emerging', its GDP rising to around $6.9 trillion, nearly 3% of the 2050 global GDP. This is not as big as any of the BRIC countries, but it will result in Mexico's economy exceeding that of the United Kingdom or France.

There are, of course, some areas where Mexico still has to make progress with regard to productivity and sustainable growth. While it is comparable to its Growth Market peers in terms of corruption and the rule of law, it is somewhat behind the high standards of South Korea (and most developed countries). Attempts by President Nieto to improve the quality of governance are likely to warrant particular attention.

Although it does score well in terms of many macroeconomic indicators, Mexico needs to perform better in a number of key categories that relate to the microeconomics of doing business: research and development, patent applications and boosting the use of personal computers and the Internet. It also has to strive to improve educational attainment for more people, including the numbers that attend full-time schooling.

If Mexico can make progress in all these areas, then the country faces a very exciting future, with an expanding and youthful population.

Indonesia

Indonesia is another country many observers frequently say should be regarded as a BRIC country, or rather a BRIIC country, with the additional 'I' for Indonesia.

Indonesia's large and young population, heading for 250 million, and its strong urbanizing trend give the country the basis for significant economic progress. By 2050 its GDP will reach $6.0 trillion, around seven to eight times bigger than today, and not much behind Mexico, according to the Goldman Sachs forecasts.

Many Indonesian policymakers say growth could be above the 5–6% predicted by these forecasts. In order to achieve their more ambitious target of 8% a year growth, though, Indonesia will have to make significant progress in key productivity and sustainable growth indicators. It needs to make progress in essentially the same areas as Mexico, but has further to go, so the policy challenge in Indonesia is all the greater.

Once more, South Korea is a shining example for Indonesia to emulate, and their shared Asian heritage might make it a bit easier to adopt some of the lessons. Governance indicators including corruption and the rule of law need attention. The forthcoming general election (due around April 2014) will be an interesting test of whether the country can transition to a style of leadership with fewer personal links between business and government, and whether the recent political stability can last. Like Mexico, Indonesia has to make positive progress in terms of educational achievement, with its current GES the lowest after India. For a country with such a young population, this is especially important.

As far as technological indicators are concerned, Indonesia currently scores very poorly, as it also does for research and development and patent applications. If its government can succeed in raising governance and educational standards, it would seem likely that existing trends and the adoption of global best practices in business and personal technologies will give Indonesia a bright future.

Nigeria

Nigeria is my favourite among the N11 countries because its people seem so full of life and hope, and because the country's potential is simply remarkable. Nigeria's demographic profile is one of the most favourable in the world. The Economist magazine estimated that by 2100 Nigeria could have 700 million people.[11] It already has 20% of the African continent's population. If Nigeria can continue down a path of reform, its potential is quite spectacular. The Goldman Sachs projections for 2050 suggest that Nigeria's economy could increase to a massive $4.9 trillion compared with its current size of $250 billion; this would mean it accounted for close to 2% of future world GDP, making it a Growth Market by any definition.

In order to realize this exciting potential, Nigeria has to undertake significant reforms. In the GES ranking, Nigeria currently sits fourteenth out of fifteen BRIC and N11 countries, nestled between Bangladesh and Pakistan. Having a large population is good news if their productivity is rising, but if productivity is stagnant, then the powerful demographics can be a burden.

However, Nigeria has clearly been heading in the right direction. Since 1997 the relative improvement in its GES has been superior to that of at least seven of the other N11 countries, although it is not yet enough to improve its ranking. Still, this is encouraging as it implies that the country can remove itself from the policy trap many emerging economies often get caught in. Visiting Seoul would be worthwhile for Nigerian leaders and policy advisors.

It is probably the three governance indicators and education that are the most important areas in which Nigeria must make progress. If the country can dramatically improve on its rule of law and corruption indicators, and the basic stability of government, and also provide basic education for its people, progress on many of the other indicators would follow.

Africa as a continent

Nigeria's future success is critical to that of the southern half of the African continent, and perhaps for the continent as a whole, as it has 20% of the total population and could easily become Africa's largest economy. This would have important consequences for many other aspects of the continent. Around the time of writing this, it is expected that formal revisions of Nigeria's national economic data could result in a better estimate of the true size of the economy, both through capturing the informal economy and, more importantly, through better measures of fast-growing new sectors like mobile telephony and Nollywood movies; these revisions could take Nigeria's economy close to that of South Africa in size.

Africa's economy collectively is about the same size as that of Russia today, and by 2050 the continent has the potential to be as big as Brazil or India in terms of GDP.[12] More trade and investment between African countries is the key to the continent achieving this potential, and Nigeria's role in this should not be underestimated. Improving the continent's basic infrastructure is obviously also a major requirement, and, in this regard, it will be interesting to see whether the declared plans for a BRIC Development Bank come to fruition, and if so, especially with South Africa's predicted role, whether this results in major infrastructure projects for southern Africa. Discussions I have enjoyed with some of those involved in the BRIC bank discussions suggest that this is a major area of focus, which could be very positive for Africa.

Turkey

Out of the blue, it seems to many of us, Turkey has gone from being an exciting and forward-looking country to one that may be going to regress. The protests in the summer of 2013, and the government's response, raise many issues, but the core question is whether or not Turkey will continue to go down a path of inclusive economic growth that allows more and more freedom and prosperity for all its citizens, irrespective of their individual political or social preferences. To continue in this vein would turn Turkey into a significant economy in the future, but of course there is great political uncertainty.

One of the UK prime minister David Cameron's first overseas visits on entering office was to Turkey, and he memorably described Turkey as being a BRIC on Europe's territory. It has mystified me for years as to why other European leaders have not realized the economic potential of Turkey. Of course, the 2013 crisis seems to have resulted in an even bigger gap between Ankara and Europe's leaders in Berlin and elsewhere, which appears to suggest that Turkish EU membership is even more distant. Certainly, if Europe is ever to escape its current economic turmoil, a change in thinking is required, one that includes embracing the importance of Turkey to European growth. Today, Turkey accounts for a little over 1% of global GDP, and its economy is more than twice the size of that of Greece. Turkey's prospects and its crisis resolution are more important than the outcome of the Greek crisis.

It will be fascinating to see how Turkey evolves after the summer protests. While its roots seem to have been very specific (objections to a new construction project in Gezi Park), in many ways the broader protests appear to be a rejection of too intrusive a government, wasted public expenditures and corruption. Just as in Brazil's mid-2013 crisis, the Turkish people have had a taste of what it is to share greater prosperity, and many want it to continue. If the government responds positively to the protests, it might be that some good will come from the situation.

Before the crisis, Turkish assets (bonds and equities) had, like others of the N11, become a darling of investors in recent years. As shown in Table 3.2, its fiscal and debt position is very similar to Mexico's, and contrasts favourably with most of the eurozone. If fiscal and other macroeconomic criteria were genuinely what mattered for the euro, policymakers in Brussels and Berlin would be begging Turkey to join the single currency, rather than making the prospect of the country's EU membership ever more distant.

Turkey's impressive macroeconomic standing is reflected in its relatively high GES. The mid-2013 protests notwithstanding, it also scores reasonably highly for education, although not at South Korean levels, which are certainly something to aim for. Linked to the crisis, Turkey still needs to make progress in terms of governance. In this sense Turkey lies behind the very high standards of the United States, or most G7 countries, and lags behind South Korea too. Interestingly, though, it does not trail in terms of governance as much as Mexico, Indonesia and Nigeria.

Beyond the weakness of governance and social upheaval, perhaps the biggest improvements necessary for Turkey's economic growth are with respect to some aspects of technology usage, research and development and patent applications. If Turkey can make good progress in those areas as well as continuing to improve its governance indicators, then it will be Europe's loss if it neglects the considerable benefits of embracing Turkey as an EU member. By 2050, Turkey's economy could be as big as $4.45 trillion, close to 2% of world GDP.

I have not yet mentioned Turkey's unique role at the geopolitical crossroads of Europe, Asia and the Middle East. The recent confrontations due to emerging public opposition to some of the policies of the AKP government, along with Turkey's proximity to Iraq, Iran and Syria, as well as to a number of ex-Soviet countries, give it a unique position in some of the world's most complex geopolitical challenges. Until mid-2013, the country also seemed to be successfully combining secular Western commercial and social attitudes with its religious beliefs. In this regard, many other countries will be watching closely to see how Turkey as a nation emerges from its current unrest.

Chapter 4

The dramatically changing face of world trade

If we had known fifteen years ago what we know now, would the European Monetary Union (EMU) ever have made any sense, even for just a few members? The case for union is much less clear than it seemed then. At the time of the EMU's creation I believed in the benefits of the single currency, but with the benefit of hindsight I might have taken a different view. This is because the patterns of world trade are so different now from how they were envisaged then. The pattern of world trade is quite different to what was expected fifteen or twenty years ago. We thought, in 1990, that intra-European trading partnerships would continue to hold most importance, but that supposition was a mistake.

The example of German exports illustrates both the scale of the reversal in the pattern of world trade, and how problematic it is for status quo thinking.

Table 4.1 shows the share of German exports to different countries in 2000 (the year after the EMU started), in 2012 and in 2020 if the trend of the past twelve years is extrapolated. German exports to the BRIC countries have risen sharply, especially to China, at the expense of the share of exports going to eurozone neighbours. On current trends, by 2020 around

Table 4.1. German exports by share (%).

	2000	2012	Change in share since 2000	2020 projected	2020 projected (half trend)
Euro area	45.5	37.5	−8.0	33.0	35.2
BRIC	3.9	11.6	7.7	23.9	16.7
France	11.3	9.5	−1.8	8.5	9.0
US	10.3	7.9	−2.4	6.6	7.2
UK	8.3	6.6	−1.6	5.7	6.2
Netherlands	6.5	6.5	−0.1	6.4	6.4
China	1.6	6.1	4.5	14.9	9.6
Austria	5.4	5.2	−0.2	5.1	5.2
N11	4.1	5.2	1.0	6.0	5.5
Italy	7.5	5.1	−2.4	3.9	4.5
Switzerland	4.3	4.4	0.2	4.6	4.5
Belgium	5.0	4.1	−1.0	3.5	3.8
Poland	2.4	3.8	1.4	5.2	4.5
Russia	1.1	3.5	2.4	7.4	5.1

Source: StBa and GSAM.

25% of total German exports will be going to the BRIC countries, with China close to twice as important as France, the most important export destination in the euro area and, of course, one of Germany's immediate neighbours. This is a remarkable development and is not at all what the founding members of the euro expected.

Germany's experience is shared with many other countries, ranging from Australia to Brazil and including many African countries. China is already the number one export market for thirty of its trading partners and this number will rise sharply in the coming years. In 2012, it overtook the United

States to become the largest trading nation in the world in terms of combined export and import of goods.

While the growth of trade with the large emerging economies, especially China, is a boon for the developed countries suffering as a result of the 2008 crisis, there is a lot of evidence that the trade between the emerging economies themselves is quite literally transformational. In the 2012 Human Development Report,[9] the UNDP found that 87% of 107 developing countries increased their trade-to-output ratios between 1990 and 2010, becoming much more connected to the world and to each other. Moreover, and perhaps of particular interest, the UNDP reported that those developing countries that

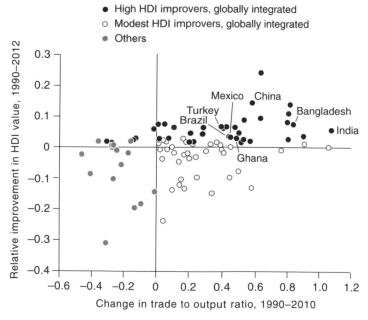

Figure 4.1. Human progress and trade expansion in the South.
Source: UN (UNDP Report, page 44).

increased their human development indices (HDIs) the most had seen outsized increases (of around 13 percentage points) in their trade-to-output ratios. Unsurprisingly, some of the biggest jumps were among the BRIC and N11 economies.

The Human Development Report highlights Brazil, China, India, Indonesia, Mexico, South Africa and Turkey, and also Bangladesh, Chile, Ghana, Mauritius, Rwanda and Tunisia, as countries that have done particularly well in terms of their overall progress in terms of their HDIs, and shows that rising trade has been both a cause and a consequence of these economic development gains.

The report goes on to illustrate the enormous change in patterns of world trade, showing that so-called 'South–South' trade tripled between 1980 and 2011, while 'North–North' trade declined. (The 'North' being defined as Australia, Canada, Japan, New Zealand, the United States and Western Europe.) Not surprisingly, 'North–South' trade also increased, but not with anything like the vigour of 'South–South' trade.

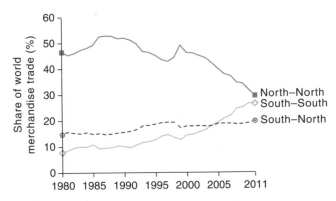

Figure 4.2. Share of world merchandise trade (%). Note: North in 1980 refers to Australia, Canada, Japan, New Zealand, the United States and Western Europe. *Source*: UN (UNDP Report, page 46).

These developments contrast with the conventional wisdom on trade. Since the 2008 credit crisis, some people have argued that the scale of the crisis might represent the beginning of the end of globalization, and a downward gear shift in global trade. This might be true for some countries in the 'North', yet both the rise of German exports to China and the other BRIC countries, and the strong growth in 'South–South' trade suggest it will not be more generally true. One paragraph from the UNDP report is striking in its description of the changes taking place in the aspirations of many emerging economies:

> Global markets have played an important role in advancing progress. All newly industrialised countries have pursued a strategy of importing what the rest of the world knows and exporting what it wants.

This is a perfect phrase to describe China's deliberate strategy from 1990 to 2010, although, as described earlier, the 'new' China is likely to be importing more from other countries in the future. The UNDP report continues:

> Without investment in people, returns from global markets are likely to be limited. Success is more likely to be the result not of a sudden opening but of gradual and sequenced integration with the world economy, according to national circumstances, and accompanied by investment in people, institutions and infrastructure.

I quoted this because assessing the future of world trade will probably depend on the achievements in economic policy, discussed in Chapter 2. How well Mexico, Indonesia, Nigeria, Turkey, the BRIC countries and the rest of the N11 nations do in terms of their people's education, their quality of governance and their infrastructure will be key. After all, the fifteen countries that make up the BRIC and N11 groups represent close to 70% of the world's population. If they make progress themselves on these various indicators, they will dominate international trade as well as accounting for a rising share of world GDP. South Korea is already a major trading nation, and the other N11 and BRIC countries are set to become so too.

Two further examples vividly illustrate the likely shift in world trade patterns between 2011 and 2020. The combined contribution from the Growth Market economies to world GDP is likely to be around three times as big as that of the G7. Their relative contribution to global trade will be at least as large, possibly even larger if some of those countries are experiencing accelerating export and import rates.

Half of this combined Growth Market contribution will come from China. China's contribution to the change in world GDP will amount to more than that of the United States and Europe put together. The other half will come from the other seven countries, so they will also contribute more than the United States plus the European Union. The N11 group is likely to contribute more to global GDP than the United States. These figures underline the shift away from 'the North' in the global economy and trade.

Figure 4.3 shows the likely pattern of growth in consumer spending in the different groups of countries. The pace of consumption growth will be particularly important for patterns of world trade. Typically, countries with high consumer spending growth tend to be important importers from the rest of the world. As can be seen, in 2011, the US dollar value of US consumption was notably higher than that of the Growth Markets, close to double that of the BRIC countries, and more than treble that of the N11. But by 2015 consumer spending in the Growth Markets is expected to be as big as that in the

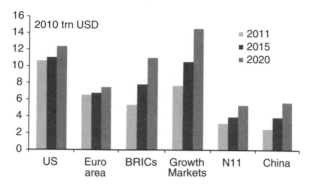

Figure 4.3. Growth Market consumption.
Source: GSAM.

United States; by 2020 it will have surpassed it. The famous American consumer will no longer be king. Exporters around the world, but especially in the United States and Europe, will have to switch their efforts to entirely different markets.

The rise of the BRIC and N11 economies, and their consumers, means that the patterns of world trade growth are set to change dramatically.

As in Germany, the most important trading partners are changing for other economies, as Tables 4.2 and 4.3 show.

The projections for 2020 assume that the trend since 2000 will continue. Of course, these trends will change at some point, but 2020 is only a few years away. The transformation of trade patterns is only one of the adjustment challenges facing the Western countries, the 'North'. There are others just as significant. In the United Kingdom and other developed nations, many people are effectively in denial about the new facts of the global economy. Although the growing importance of China and the other BRIC countries and Growth Markets is appreciated, it is often seen as something that will

Table 4.2. North: major export markets.

	2000	2012	2020	2020 (half trend)
US	Canada (23%)	Canada (19%)	Canada (17%)	Canada (18%)
	Mexico (14%)	Mexico (14%)	China (16%)	Mexico (14%)
	Japan (8%)	China (7%)	Mexico (14%)	China (11%)
UK	US (16%)	US (14%)	US (13%)	US (13%)
	Germany (12%)	Germany (11%)	Germany (10%)	Germany (10%)
	France (10%)	Netherlands (8%)	China (10%)	Netherlands (8%)
Germany	France (11%)	France (10%)	China (15%)	China (10%)
	US (10%)	US (8%)	France (8%)	France (9%)
	UK (8%)	UK (7%)	Russia (7%)	US (7%)
Japan	US (30%)	China (18%)	China (36%)	China (26%)
	Taiwan (7%)	US (18%)	US (12%)	US (15%)
	Korea (6%)	Korea (8%)	Russia (9%)	Korea (8%)

Calculated by extrapolating the trends in a country's export destination shares. *Source*: GSAM.

take effect at some point in the future, whereas it is a current reality.

The sooner the fact of the global shift is understood, the sooner a new and more effective set of institutions for global governance can come about.

Table 4.3. South: major export markets.

	2000	2012	2020	2020 (half trend)
Brazil	US (24%)	China (17%)	China (71%)	China (36%)
	Argentina (11%)	US (11%)	India (7%)	US (9%)
	Netherlands (5%)	Argentina (7%)	Netherlands (7%)	Netherlands (7%)
Russia	Germany (9%)	Netherlands (12%)	Netherlands (30%)	Netherlands (19%)
	Italy (7%)	China (6%)	China (8%)	China (7%)
	Italy (7%)	Italy (6%)	Italy (5%)	Italy (5%)
India	US (19%)	US (13%)	UAE (20%)	UAE (16%)
	UAE (6%)	UAE (12%)	US (9%)	US (11%)
	Hong Kong (6%)	China (5%)	China (9%)	China (7%)
China	US (21%)	US (17%)	US (15%)	US (16%)
	Hong Kong (18%)	Hong Kong (14%)	Hong Kong (12%)	Hong Kong (13%)
	Japan (17%)	Japan (8%)	Africa (6%)	Japan (6%)

Calculated by extrapolating the trends in a country's export destination shares. *Source*: GSAM.

Chapter 5

The BRIC road to growth

It is now twelve years since I wrote a report for Goldman Sachs entitled 'Building better global economic BRICs'.[13] Today, it is still – perhaps unfortunately – the case that the world needs better economic BRICs.

In that 2001 paper, I focused on two main issues. First, the rise of Brazil, Russia, India and China and their global influence – this is the issue that has become so well known. The second issue was why, as a result of the rise in global influence of these countries, the world needed much better global economic governance. This included, I argued then, the need for the member countries of the euro to behave as one, with genuinely unified economic governance. Most focus back then was, of course, on the BRIC story, especially after my 2003 paper 'Dreaming with BRICs: the path to 2050'.[14] Too little attention has been paid to the question of the world's economic governance. By now, everyone knows about the BRIC phenomenon, but few people truly understand the degree to which the world has already changed and continues to change rapidly. Global governance has inched in the right direction with the advent of the G20, but international bodies and forums continue to reflect the old pattern of global economic power. This needs to change, significantly and soon.

This chapter turns to the governance question, starting with the eurozone. Until this is run effectively, it will be difficult to get a better structure for wider global governance, or to make the appropriate room for China, the other BRIC countries and perhaps also other rising economies.

The European conundrum

The eurozone crisis is not really a sovereign debt crisis, nor is it really an economic crisis in many ways. Clearly, some eurozone members had (and still have) levels of government debt that were far too high, but they are not unique in this regard. It is also clear that some eurozone countries had, at the start of the crisis, a very uncompetitive economy with high labour costs. Yet if one country is measured as uncompetitive, it is relative to another country. As the charts and tables below illustrate, the eurozone debt position measured as a weighted average of its members is actually better than in other parts of the developed world, while the competitive mismatch between different eurozone members against each other has narrowed sharply in the past couple of years.

Table 5.1 shows the cyclically adjusted fiscal balance of some of the developed economies, including eurozone members, their net debt-to-GDP position, and their GESs.

The cyclically adjusted fiscal balance refers to the probable level of the government deficit if the economy had been growing at its normal trend. As most developed economies have grown below trend since the recovery from the 2008 crisis (if they have grown at all), their actual reported fiscal deficits are higher than these cyclically adjusted deficits. But the cyclically adjusted balance is a fairer reflection of the true stance of fiscal policy. As can be seen, on this measure, the

Table 5.1. Who is fit for the EMU?

	Cyclically adjusted budget deficit (%GDP)	Gross general government debt (%GDP)	GES
Germany	0.0	80.4	7.1
France	−1.9	92.7	6.7
Italy	−0.2	130.6	5.7
Spain	−4.2	91.8	6.1
Netherlands	−1.2	74.5	7.6
Belgium	−2.1	100.3	7.0
Austria	−1.6	74.2	6.9
Greece	0.2	179.5	4.8
Finland	−0.5	56.9	7.4
Ireland	−5.5	122.0	6.4
Portugal	−3.0	122.3	5.8
Slovakia	−2.4	55.3	6.2
EMU average	−1.4	95.0	6.8
UK	−4.3	93.6	6.7
US	−4.6	108.1	6.8
Canada	−2.1	87.0	7.1
Japan	−9.5	245.4	6.6
Australia	−1.1	27.6	7.6
Sweden	−0.9	37.7	7.6

Source: IMF and GSAM.
Debt and deficit figures are 2013 estimates.

eurozone is doing considerably better than the United Kingdom or the United States, and dramatically better than Japan. Italy actually shows a cyclically adjusted *surplus*, the best fiscal position within the G7. If the eurozone were purely suffering

from a fiscal crisis, sovereign bond yields would be a lot higher in the countries with the worst fiscal positions.

Turning to the levels of outstanding debt, what is striking is that so many developed countries have extremely high levels of public debt, but the average eurozone position is not exceptionally poor by these general standards. Once more, Japan stands out as being especially disturbing, but the average of the eurozone area is not that different from that of the United States or the United Kingdom.

One conclusion from the first two columns of Table 5.1 might be that the eurozone should not have included all the existing member countries that it has, which would certainly be a widely shared view. However, the third column departs from the conventional diagnosis by showing that the GESs, indicating growth and productivity potential, are more relevant than generally perceived. On this measure, the average eurozone performance compares reasonably well with the other G7 countries, although it does not score the highest. What is also clear is that some countries at the centre of the financial crisis have very low scores. This suggests that they have a sustainable growth problem, which in itself may be the cause of their debt problems, and of course raises reasonable questions as to whether these countries should have been allowed into the eurozone to start with. What it clearly indicates is that if all these countries are to be able to remain in a monetary union, and for it to be a credible and sustainable one, euro area policymakers need a *pan*-euro-area policy framework.

Table 5.2 shows the same three variables for the eight Growth Market economies. It shows a quite remarkable contrast to Table 5.1. The cyclically adjusted fiscal balance and the outstanding debt position of the Growth Eight (those eight emerging economies that are currently more than 1% of global GDP) show a degree of fiscal conservatism that the cautious

Table 5.2. Could the Growth Eight join the EMU?

	Cyclically adjusted budget deficit (%GDP)	Gross general government debt (%GDP)	GES
Brazil	−2.7	67.2	3.9
India	−8.8	66.4	5.4
Mexico	−3.7	43.5	5.1
Turkey	−1.6	35.5	5.2
Korea	2.3	32.5	7.9
Indonesia	−1.4	23.6	4.8
China	−0.9	21.3	5.5
Russia	0.5	10.4	5.3

Source: IMF and GSAM.
Debt and deficit figures are 2013 estimates.

Germans would be proud of. The original Maastricht Criteria for euro membership were a cyclically adjusted deficit of 3% of GDP or less, and an outstanding debt-to-GDP ratio of 60% or less. India would be the only one of the Growth Eight that would fail to meet both of these tough criteria, which are rarely ever satisfied by the euro members themselves.

It is also the case that the Growth Market economies generally have much weaker GESs than the developed countries, although not as weak as the weakest of these, such as Greece. South Korea, as described earlier, sets an example for most of the developed world.

What these contrasting tables highlight is the mismatch between global governance structures and basic economic criteria. Should the leadership of the IMF and World Bank still lie with countries with weak fiscal and debt positions, making little contribution to global growth?

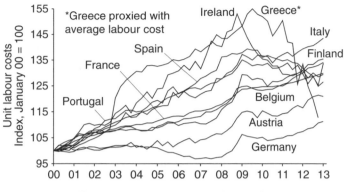

Figure 5.1. Unit labour costs (Europe).

Returning to the euro area, Figure 5.1 shows the changing relative position of competitiveness in terms of the main member countries measured by their unit labour costs.

During the first decade of the euro's existence, there was a sharp deterioration in the competitive position of a number of member countries, notably Greece, Italy and Ireland, compared with Germany. What is less well appreciated is that, in the last couple of years, many of them have shown considerable improvements. Italy currently stands out as the weakest in terms of competitiveness. However, the chart says little about whether the improving competitiveness of some eurozone countries will be at the expense of Germany or the rest of the world instead. Improving their internal competitiveness might be useful, but the region as a whole needs to improve its aggregate position relative to the rest of the world. As the euro itself is trading in the currency markets at a value that is above most observers' judgement about its competitive level, this suggests that the aggregate competitive position of the eurozone is deteriorating despite the improved internal competitiveness.

One of the reasons for this is that, despite all the per-ceived problems, the euro area has both a slight trade and current account surplus with the rest of the world. Figure 5.2 shows both the total euro area current account balance and the 'broader' basic balance (adding the net balance in foreign direct investments and net cross border portfolio flows in bonds and equities to the current account balance). Seen in this manner, perhaps it is unusual for the euro area to have been experiencing a crisis, given that it has a small balance of payments surplus. For most of my professional experience, crises usually occur when countries or regions suffer from bal-ance of payments current account or basic deficits. It is this fact that makes me think that from a purely economic per-spective this is an unnecessary crisis, and that the euro area's real problems are in its design and governance.

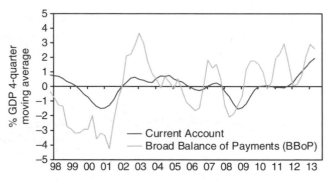

Figure 5.2. Euro area current account.

Euro area governance

The core question around the euro is whether or not it is an optimal currency zone. Some people have always doubted the sustainability of the euro. More, including myself at times, have questioned its wisdom for such a diverse group of countries. But given that they did all join, the only way to ensure the sustainability of all countries' membership, and the future of the euro itself, was for them to align their economic policies fully. Arguably, this is exactly what happens for monetary matters with the European Central Bank (ECB), the euro area's central bank. However, when it comes to non-monetary matters, each member still acts in accordance with domestic priorities and not primarily under its obligations towards the eurozone.

One way in which euro area countries could persuade financial markets that their economic policies are as one, and to demonstrate their unity, would be for members to abandon their individual representation in international economic forums, including each of the G7, G8, the IMF and the World Bank, standing instead behind a single eurozone seat. Without the euro area members shifting in this way, it is difficult to see how we can get better and more effective global governance.

The role of BRICs in global governance

By the end of 2015, possibly earlier, the BRIC countries will be collectively bigger than the United States, and China will be considerably bigger than all the G7 economies apart from the United States, more than double the size of any of the European G7 countries. Is it either realistic or sustainable for China and the other BRIC countries not to have a bigger role in global governance? The answer to this question was already clear some years ago, and their collective share of global GDP has since reached approximately 20%.

The elevated importance of the G20 since the global economic crisis in 2008 has helped bring the BRIC countries into a more central role in global policymaking. In a 2004 report I co-authored with Robert Hormats, we advocated an enhanced role for the G20.[15] The G20 is indeed a significantly more representative group than either the G7 or the G8. I argued in 2001 that the G7 should be replaced by an expanded G9, in which each of the four BRIC countries (but not including South Africa) would be included and the eurozone members would be represented as one by the Euro Group. In 2004, Hormats and I argued the case for a 'Financial 8' or an 'F8', with China to be added to the existing G7 countries, reflecting its crucial presence in most key financial matters.

Would an expanded role for the G20, with the Growth Market economies all included, be sufficient for better and fairer global governance? It certainly seems more representative but, as any participant in a G20 meeting might tell you, it has proven difficult for such a large group to work effectively. In fact, the G20 involves more than twenty countries, and, while it clearly satisfies a goal of legitimacy, it is difficult to see how it can satisfy the desire for greater effectiveness or optimality of policymaking. The sheer number of people present in any room at a G20 meeting makes effective discussion and decision-making challenging, and many participants often complain about such meetings becoming bureaucratic and formulaic in nature. Many G7 members have confided to me that this frustration with the G20 procedure has, ironically, contributed to a new lease of life at their own G7. Some of the G7 members also think that, while it is conceptually important that a G20 forum now exists, where the BRIC countries are present, they should not have an increased role and importance in decision-making. Some of the BRIC participants realize that their presence is not necessarily welcomed by the global decision-making body.

Practical constraints aside, the existence of the G20 gives *some* greater legitimacy to the structures of global economic governance. Perhaps it will also become more effective as a decision-making body over time.

Still, within the G20, a smaller and more effective decision-making body should be encouraged. There are four questions concerning global governance. First, would it be appropriate to no longer include the United Kingdom or Canada? Second, in reality, is it practical to remove countries from important international governance bodies given all the procedural and complex diplomatic issues involved? Third, is there a case for inclusion of each BRIC country in the narrower group? Fourth, is it practical to give the rising emerging economies a bigger and more representative role in the IMF and the World Bank?

Starting with the first of these, the presence of the United Kingdom and Canada is a remnant of the earlier global economic order; but, in terms of the size of their economies today, the case for their inclusion in the bodies of global policymaking is questionable. Canada is smaller than each of the BRIC countries, and comparable to either Australia or Spain in size, neither of which is part of the G7. Canada borders the United States, is an important producer of commodities and a valuable, experienced member of the international community. Whether this is sufficient in the new complex global order is quite debatable, and anyway the same points could be made about Australia. For the United Kingdom, similar arguments hold, and of course the United Kingdom is considerably larger than Canada and an important financial centre, but does it have any more legitimate presence in the new world than Brazil, an economy of similar size but – the last two years excepted – growing far faster?

Secondly, there is a clear need for global governance organizations to be both more robust and flexible as well as more representative. There is a tendency for new 'G' groups to be created primarily to respond to specific crises of that moment, and then to continue to exist in name while ceasing to have any real purpose. The G20 itself faces the risk of such a fate. One way of thinking about this dilemma is to borrow an idea from football, and consider the notion of promotion and relegation from a given group. A nation could be elevated to the group if its GDP exceeded that of an existing member, which would be 'relegated' to make room. It is quite conceivable that this might allow a more effective central G7 entity to preside over global governance within a wider umbrella framework, although it would require objective guidelines. Some objective set of indicators established and maintained by the IMF, based on GDP, population, sustainability of growth and changes in each of these would need to be clearly established to meet such a challenging goal.

On the remaining two issues, in order to give the BRIC countries (and other large emerging economies) their representative weight, some other countries will have to give up their representation. The obvious, and perhaps only, move is for the eurozone members to have a sole representative. As discussed, this would help the euro to regain its credibility and it would be helpful for the wider governance group as well. China could then join a narrower group with the United States, Japan and the euro area (or perhaps the European Union as a whole). Not only do the eurozone countries share a common currency, they are in relative decline in the world economy. This step would simultaneously send a clear statement concerning commitment to the euro, and create room for BRICs and other countries to be given their due voice in the G groups, the IMF and the World Bank.

Is it justifiable to create more space for the BRIC countries in international governance? The answer partly depends on whether they are prepared to play a more responsible role in global governance. Some of the countries are happy to be recognized as being more important but do not want to be obligated by the greater responsibility that would come with increased weight in global organizations. China clearly needs to step up to the increased responsibility that goes with its scale and importance. China's role within the BRICs' own political grouping may be revealing, both as to whether they are moving towards acceptance of this responsibility, and as to whether the BRIC countries collectively are likely to be a more effective force.

When I created the BRIC acronym, I did not then imagine that it would ever develop into a political club. Moreover, despite having their large scale in common, the BRIC countries share little else. They have quite varying degrees of per capita incomes, two are not democracies, while three are major commodity producers and two are major commodity importers. These differences perhaps explain why the countries had not really succeeded in achieving a common purpose before the Durban Summit of March 2013 (this, of course, including South Africa as well as the original four, and so a 'BRICS', with the added 'S', rather than a 'BRIC' summit). But with the announcement then of the plan to develop the BRICS Development Bank, this may herald the beginning of a new era. They could not have reached this decision without China showing a clear commitment, which I believe to be potentially very important, as this is one of the first signs that Beijing has decided to actively support a collective BRIC purpose. While it is dangerous to extrapolate from this single decision, it might signal the beginning of China playing a significant role on the bigger global stage. This, along with the need for the eurozone countries to act as one, is one of the key shifts necessary for a more effective, as well as legitimate, form of global governance.

The BRIC Development Bank

At their Durban meeting, the BRIC leaders carried through on their previous stated intention to launch a joint BRIC Development Bank. They provided no details about its planned location, its capital or its organization, but indicated that they will follow through with its creation. This was an important symbolic moment, as previous BRIC meetings had been mainly ceremonial with specific policy steps generally confined to bilateral currency swap deals, in which countries would announce measures to facilitate more trade with each other. The establishment of a joint development bank is a bigger move and demonstrates, at least in principle, that this group can take effective decisions.

As for the likely location of its headquarters, I can imagine three possibilities. Within the BRIC countries, it would seem that only China or South Africa would be probable or suitable, China because of its size and importance. It would be difficult for Brazil, India or Russia to argue that one of their cities should be the host, as it would be unclear what advantage they would offer relative to each other. Conversely, South Africa might make a sensible choice precisely because it is much smaller than any of the BRIC countries and headquartering the bank in South Africa would help cement its inclusion in the club. South Africa's financial sector is quite advanced, and the country can act as a financial gateway to the rest of the African continent. If there is competitive opposition from within the BRIC countries to either of these, I often find myself thinking that London might be a practical choice as a compromise, reflecting London's role as a world financial centre and, of course, its highly favourable central time zone.

The initial steps to capitalize the bank will also be another important sign of its likely practical importance. Either the members could agree that each country's capital commitment should reflect its relative GDP size, in which case China would contribute the same as the other four put together. The downside to this option is that it would confirm a very high degree of Chinese influence. Some could argue that the relative capital contribution should be more reflective of each country's income per capita rather than its absolute size, in which case Brazil and Russia would then be likely to contribute proportionally more, and South Africa and India the least. Alternatively, the countries could choose to make equal capital contributions. At the time of the Durban meeting, there were rumours that they had agreed a capital contribution of $10 billion each, for a total of $50 billion. This has not been confirmed, but neither has it been categorically denied. A $10 billion commitment from South Africa, representing around 2.5% of its GDP, would be a bigger fiscal burden for them than it would for China at less than 0.1% of its GDP. Perhaps this alternative would be particularly logical if South Africa were also chosen as the headquarters, as then it would give them a defined purpose as a BRICS member given some of the reservations some might have based on their much smaller size than the others as an economy.

What will the BRIC bank do?

Linked to where the bank will be headquartered and how it is initially capitalized is the critical issue of its actual purpose and goals. Presumably, it will be to support and drive forward key shared development projects, especially, but not only, in trade and infrastructure. Brazil and South Africa do not share borders with any other BRIC country and, in that regard, joint physical infrastructure projects with other BRIC countries might not be useful or meaningful. India and Russia have extensive borders with China, so one can easily think of shared energy-based infrastructure projects between them, for example, or joint project financing for water projects. But any of these infrastructure projects would be primarily of a bilateral nature, and arguably served better by being undertaken by their own national development banks.

Where the BRIC bank might be more truly useful and effective would be in areas that relate to boosting the countries' shared trade and economic development in sectors of their economies and society that need to make progress. In Chapter 2, I discussed how much emerging countries could learn from South Korea's example. Each of the BRIC countries faces problems in specific areas, and shared initiatives could bring real benefits, not least because they would apply peer pressure for each BRIC country to follow through on commitments. Three different areas stand out as candidates.

Firstly, while the adoption of mobile telephony is now quite widespread in each of the BRIC countries, the usage and application of other new technologies are not. Looking at how successful South Korea has been in these areas, technology investments would be a highly beneficial project focus for the BRIC Development Bank.

Secondly, and in the same spirit, although harder to achieve, educational enhancement for the population of the BRIC countries is a shared need. India would seem to have the greatest absolute need at each level of primary, secondary and tertiary education, with rural South Africa perhaps the next most pressing. Brazil, China and Russia are all trying to improve their educational standards, although their individual needs are rather different. In 2001 and 2002, after the bursting of the bubble in so-called TMT stocks (technology, media and telecommunications), the then Goldman Sachs CEO Hank Paulson established a GS 'purpose' committee. Some of us proposed the idea of supporting the development of a top class university in Africa. It was seen, understandably, as too radical or ambitious a project for us to implement, or perhaps to be accepted by government officials. I think it would make a lot of sense for a shared commitment by BRIC countries to develop world class universities in each of them. According to the well-respected Shanghai rankings,[7] in their 2012 ranking of the top 100 universities, there was only one (Moscow State) located in any of the BRIC countries. Given that they are already responsible for more than 20% of world GDP, this number should be higher. Of the top 500 ranking, there are around 35, many of them from China, but this is still quite low for their share of global GDP.

A second lesson from South Korea, in an even more challenging area than education, concerns governance in the BRIC countries, particularly tackling the nature and scale of corruption, and improving the rule of law. It would be extremely helpful in raising standards and aspirations in these countries to link the governance issue to improvements in tertiary education. Early in 2013, a leading Nigerian policymaker said to me that the economics of corruption are much more complex than most commentators suggest. He argued that there could be some instances in which such practices could be tolerable if they contributed to broader gains for society. It is not obvious to me that ultimately such examples will be significant or desirable, but the issues need to be studied more carefully in poorer developing societies, not least to avoid the counterproductive impression of preaching. A BRIC Development Bank would be in a very good position to finance such research and to ensure it is studied in centres of learning.

When it comes to more conventional projects for the BRIC bank, it is certainly easy to conceive of the case for shared financing in many projects relating to commodities, especially energy usage, and, within it, efficiency-enhancing technologies and alternative, less polluting energies. As Brazil, Russia and South Africa are all major commodity producers, and China and India are likely to become increasingly large consumers of natural resources, the case for shared project financing in this vast field is clear. Brief analysis of global climate change discussions reveals that there has often been a split between the more advanced nations and the large developing ones, primarily because their goals differ. The emerging economies, aspiring to similar standards of living to those enjoyed by the richest nations, believe that their ambitions for higher levels of income must be at least acknowledged, whereas the more advanced countries primarily focus on the consequences for aggregate demand and prices, as well as for emissions, of their rising energy usage. While there are income differences between the BRIC countries, these are considerably smaller than the differences between their incomes and those of larger, more advanced nations, and a goal of achieving shared interests in energy development and its consequences should be more feasible.

Chapter 6

The challenge for the United Kingdom

I have often found myself at a bit of a loss to explain why the UK economy has struggled so much to recover from the 2008 crisis. Having made the decision to not join the euro in its first decade, in contrast to most of continental Europe, the United Kingdom had the potential benefit of a considerable decline in the value of sterling against many currencies, the euro included (see Figure 6.1). The resulting improvement in competitiveness (the price of British goods having declined in other currencies) should have allowed the United Kingdom to gain export market share at the expense of many other developed countries. While the government's strong stance on debt reduction and public spending restraint may be an obvious reason for muted growth in domestic demand, a sharp decline in the currency of a country pursuing fiscal constraint is a classic textbook recipe for successful economic adjustment.

Among the problems of trying to understand the post-2008 UK economy remains the accuracy of UK GDP data. A number of analysts sometimes question its accuracy, and often think it has been underestimating the level of GDP. For example, Kevin Daly, the chief UK economist at Goldman

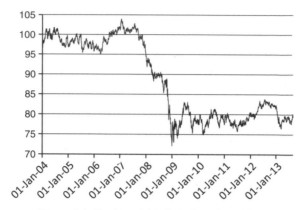

Figure 6.1. Trade weighted sterling since 2007.
Source: GS Global ECS Research.

Sachs, calculates that since 1986, two years after the first estimate from the ONS, the average revision to the first real GDP
estimate has been ±0.47, with many of the revisions higher
than this. He also found evidence that the initial UK estimate
was statistically less accurate than that of many other developed economies.[16] Before 2008, this underestimate would
not normally have been big enough to be relevant, but in
the weak-growth environment and the politically complex
coalition situation since 2010, a consistently inaccurate GDP
estimate adds to the rather charged debate around economic policy. For example, during 2012 and early 2013, there was
enormous focus on the issue of a so-called double-dip recession, as a short recovery from negative growth was followed
by a return to two consecutive quarters of GDP contraction
(technically, the basis for declaring the economy in recession).
Following revisions in June 2013, there were in fact no longer
two consecutive negative quarters in 2012, so there was no
official second recession after all.

Things have become even more complicated since the June revisions, which now suggest that the decline in GDP from so-called peak to trough was even bigger in 2009, now some 7.2% instead of 6.9%, leaving the economy still 3.9% weaker than its pre-crisis levels. If this is the final story, which is doubtful, it suggests that the pre-2008 tendency to underestimate actual GDP has now been replaced by a more balanced tendency for large revisions both upwards and downwards. I suspect this is not likely to be the final judgement, and it makes discussion about what exactly is going on in the economy very difficult for all concerned.

Perhaps a function of the sheer ubiquity of modern media, the government appears to find it difficult to step above the frenzied intensity of any topical event, and often rushes to make quick judgement. I have found myself frequently refer-ring to this as 'the Facebook crisis', as it is often difficult to distinguish between emotional reactions to events played out in instant debates, and a more sober, objective reflec-tion. In this emotional environment, the difference between an initial estimate of −0.1% quarterly GDP growth and a later revised +0.1% estimate is not unimportant in terms of its influ-ence on policymakers and the political 'blame game'. In reality, though, the difference between −0.1% and +0.1% is essentially meaningless.

Notwithstanding the last point, the coalition government in its first three years of office has stuck with two broad eco-nomic strategies: to reduce the level of government debt rela-tive to GDP, and to reduce the importance of the banking sec-tor in terms of its overall share in GDP. While both goals are necessary, to have applied them with the tenacity in which policymakers did at the same time might explain why the UK recovery was so disappointing in 2010–12. Mistaken tactics with regard to these two goals may help explain the United Kingdom's continuing economic weakness.

There are some who believe that the coalition's strategy would have borne much greater fruit had it not been for the scale of the eurozone crisis and the consequent weakness in the United Kingdom's major export markets. But, anyway, a twin strategy of fiscal restraint and forced retrenchment of the banking sector would have required a substantial positive stimulus to offset the effects on growth. With respect to the government's strategy on debt reduction, there is little evidence that it has achieved any measure of success. It is almost definitely the case that weak or flat real GDP growth is likely to cause government debt to rise, although it is also probably true that the causality runs both ways, and highly indebted economies will struggle to grow as much as those that are less burdened. It is important to remember that the UK coalition government was formed on the same May 2010 weekend that the Greek financial crisis initially erupted in a way that suggested there could be contagious consequences elsewhere, such that other countries with rapidly rising debt might lose the confidence of markets. For a coalition that probably did not expect to be thrown together, the appeal of being determined to put debt reduction at the centre of its policies was perhaps especially strong, as it would serve as a constant reminder to the public that the high level of debt was a result of the previous Labour government's policies.

In addition to the domestic political appeal, there is a body of economic research that seems to show that debt reduction, especially when executed through expenditure restraint, is ultimately successful in promoting growth. The now famous research was conducted by Carmen Reinhart and Kenneth Rogoff.[17,18] In April 2013, a follow-up by economists at the University of Massachusetts raised some doubts about the robustness of the Rogoff and Reinhart thesis.[19] The Rogoff and Reinhart analysis became an attractive justification for policymakers eager to embark on a strategy of debt reduction, perhaps with more confidence than the academic work would really support. The Reinhart–Rogoff argument, based on many historical examples – and the aggregation of research across countries – suggested that once debt moves above 90% of GDP, economic growth will weaken. The Massachusetts study, partly by discovering an error in the Reinhart and Rogoff study, suggested that growth is probably not so sensitive to a specific level of government debt, although the correlation between higher debt and slower growth remains clear. Weak or no economic growth, as many developed economies have experienced since 2008, results in much higher debt-to-GDP ratios as tax revenues and government spending – on unemployment benefits and the like – rise. It is also true that rising debt, especially if not due to a recession, can cause economies to weaken, not least because private sector agents worry about future rising tax burdens and/or government expenditure cuts. But it is obviously hard to be precise about the degree to which this is the case.

Just as obvious is that the experience of country X is highly unlikely to be the same as that of country Y; of course different countries have different experiences. For example, are Greek and Japanese debt levels driven by the same forces? Is the growth of Japanese debt due more to inappropriate spending and tax policies or to the absence of real GDP growth for twenty years? If, instead of growing by just 1% over the last twenty years, Japan had continued to grow at the 4.5% average of the previous twenty years, its debt-to-GDP ratio would be considerably lower. In the case of Greece, it would seem that a sustained period of inappropriate fiscal policies can be held more responsible. What is more, in many of the 'successful' examples of debt reduction and government spending restraint, there is usually scope for a significant monetary policy – compensation allowing lower interest rates and a lower exchange rate to offset the fiscal restraint. While the United Kingdom has benefited in principle from the exchange rate factor, it has not enjoyed the traditional monetary policy offset.

This brings me to the second strand of the current UK government's policy in its first three years: its attitude towards the banking industry. Banks play a key role in transmitting the consequence of a change in the central bank's monetary policies. Therefore, when the central bank is embarking on a non-traditional form of monetary policy, as the Bank of England, like many other central banks, has done, it is more difficult to realize the desired effects if the banks are not allowed to behave as 'normal'. UK policymakers have not thought carefully enough about this issue, particularly against the backdrop of desired fiscal restraint and, crucially, the United Kingdom's net added value to the rest of the world.

The often implicit, but occasionally explicit, goal of reducing the size of the banking sector in relation to overall GDP is potentially misplaced in itself and confused with the clearer and more sensible goal of having a better-regulated financial sector. Much of the City of London's activity involves commercial overseas firms involved in commerce and trade with the rest of the world. Its aggregate activity contributes both to UK GDP and significantly to the UK's balance of payments.

While UK banks play a role in the City, it is not a dominant one, and in this context the appropriate regulatory and capital requirements for the domestic activities of UK banks should not be confused with the appropriate environment for many financial institutions operating in the City, many of which have domestic obligations to their home country, and are regulated accordingly.

In the immediate aftermath of the 2008 crisis a number of G20 policymakers, including those in the United Kingdom, appeared to articulate the case for the introduction of clear, centralized capital rules for banks. Specifically, they would be guided by regulation requiring higher buffers of capital to be built up during times of economic buoyancy, which would allow them to call on such capital during less healthy economic periods. This principle seemed both sensible and reasonably easy to apply. In its place, the United Kingdom and others have since introduced policies aimed at forcing banks to raise even higher amounts of capital, without acknowledging either their critical role in the monetary transmission mechanism or the fact that the weak economy constrains the actions of banks.

UK exports in the changing world

As discussed earlier, in one sense it is mystifying that UK exports have not increased more, given the considerable depreciation of the pound since 2008. The government argues that the main reason for this disappointment is the eurozone crisis, given the euro area's importance as an importer of UK goods and services. The euro area absorbs 45% of total UK exports. The eurozone crisis and the subsequent recession in many member economies will clearly have affected UK exports.

However, that cannot be the whole explanation. Firstly, within the eurozone, the biggest UK markets are not the countries in crisis. Germany itself accounts for around 25% of UK exports to the eurozone. Secondly, as always, it is

Table 6.1. UK exports to various destinations.

	2000	2012	Change in share since 2000	2020 projected	2020 projected (half trend)
Euro area	54.6%	44.7%	−9.9%	39.2%	41.9%
US	15.6%	13.7%	−1.9%	12.5%	13.1%
Germany	12.1%	10.8%	−1.3%	10.0%	10.4%
Netherlands	8.1%	8.3%	0.2%	8.5%	8.4%
BRIC	2.6%	7.8%	5.2%	16.1%	11.3%
France	9.9%	7.0%	−2.9%	5.5%	6.2%
Irish Republic	6.6%	5.8%	−0.8%	5.3%	5.6%
Belgium/ Luxembourg	5.5%	4.9%	−0.6%	4.5%	4.7%
N11	3.3%	4.6%	1.3%	5.7%	5.1%
China	0.8%	3.5%	2.7%	9.6%	5.9%
Spain	4.4%	2.8%	−1.6%	2.1%	2.4%
Italy	4.5%	2.7%	−1.8%	1.9%	2.3%
Switzerland	1.7%	2.2%	0.6%	2.7%	2.5%
Sweden	2.2%	1.9%	−0.3%	1.7%	1.8%
Russia	0.4%	1.9%	1.5%	5.6%	3.3%

important to not confuse levels of economic indicators with the rate of change. While the eurozone accounts for 45% of UK exports, this is nearly 10% *less* than in 2000, as Table 6.1 shows. The eurozone is a whole fifth less important for UK exporters than it was twenty years ago. Over that period, China, the BRIC countries collectively and the N11 have become significantly more important for UK exporters. Given that the pound's exchange rate has weakened, the disappointing export performance can only be ascribed either to weakness in demand in all export markets or to having the wrong products to satisfy the markets where demand is growing most, or to a combination of the two. As can be seen in Table 6.1, if this same trend continues for the rest of this decade, the euro-zone's importance as an export market will decline further and China's importance will increase significantly. Of course, there is little that the United Kingdom can do to influence the level of demand in overseas economies, but it can focus on what it tries to export to them. Here, again, the issue of financial services, and especially the role played by UK banks, is key. Given the fortuitous nature of the convenient UK time zone, the continued rise in the use of the English language for conducting business, and the smooth functioning of UK labour markets and the legal system, the country should not discourage the role of the City. On the contrary, it should aim to support its continued success, although it must better insulate its domestic financial system from any future shocks due to the global activities its own or other banks might undertake. Other related services such as the legal profession and accounting and consultancy services are areas where the United Kingdom is likely to have a continued, and possibly improving, advantage over other countries. As the Growth Markets become more prosperous, it is quite likely that they will demand more of what the United Kingdom can offer in terms of these intangible services.

In the emotive atmosphere since the 2008 crisis, a natural corollary to seeking a smaller financial services sector has been an aim to grow the manufacturing sector. While this is understandable on an emotional and historical basis, it is a strategy that involves some risks, not least the fact that the United Kingdom could not quickly or easily catch up with the leading manufacturing nations. Germany has been a successful exporting manufacturer for most of the post-World War II period, and within Asia both South Korea and Japan have had considerable industrial success. A weaker pound will help the United Kingdom, and over time will probably benefit industrial exports. In this regard, the recent success of UK auto exports is an encouraging example, and supports those that believe there is nothing inherently unproductive about the United Kingdom. Over the past two years, the United Kingdom has moved into a small trade surplus in auto exports – something it had not achieved in the previous thirty years. Given that the location of auto production is highly sensitive to exchange rates, this evidence suggests that at least some industries are benefiting from the decline of sterling since 2008.

In terms of other industries, though, the United Kingdom will need to focus on areas where it really does have some kind of natural edge compared with other successful exporting nations. One area that seems a likely winner in this sense is modern lifestyle and medical technologies, especially those emerging from British universities. Here, again, the rise in the use of spoken English is a natural advantage to exploit.

Indeed, shifting back towards services, the United Kingdom could capitalize on its educational sector commercially both directly, through exports, and indirectly, by forming closer ties with emerging economic powers. The rise of affluent families in many Middle Eastern and Asian countries offers a very fertile market. I have come across many personal anecdotes during my travels. For example, at a dinner in Singapore, one person told me that as a result of the pound's decline and the strength of the Australian dollar, more citizens there were choosing the United Kingdom as a destination to send their children for tertiary education. Given the wealth of Singaporeans, one would imagine that for aspiring parents elsewhere in the emerging world the relative cost would play an even bigger role. The only obstacle is the coalition government's wish to be tough on immigration to appease domestic voters, although it is hard to see the short-term stays of students as a major contributor to voters' concerns about immigration.

So it would seem to be the case that the future export opportunities for the United Kingdom are both diverse and perhaps brighter than often imagined. Whether they are sufficient to help bring about a more substantial and sustainable level of overall GDP growth is less clear; as I have argued here, this will also require more careful thought about domestic policies.

Chapter 7

Rescuing capitalism

Has capitalism reached the end of the road?

It has become common since the 2008 crisis for some people to react against market capitalism, but the debate needs to be more nuanced. We should neither be writing off capitalism nor defending a particular model of capitalism. In the autumn of 2012, I attended a lunch at a well-known right-of-centre think tank to participate in a discussion about whether capitalism was broken or not. Some very prominent British thinkers and policymakers were present, and after hearing some of their views I realized that my perspective on the crisis and the changing world is very different to the received wisdom. The essence of the discussion was that the 2008 crisis had destroyed the version of capitalism that my host had passionately believed in, which in his mind originated with Thatcherism in the United Kingdom and Reaganomics in the United States. In my view, though, the reality is that capitalism adjusts depending on events, and what people want, and that this is true whether we are talking about formal democracies or not. Clearly, in the United Kingdom and much of the rest of the world, if an elected government either fails to deliver what the electorate hoped for, or presides over a dreadful crisis, we usually throw them out and elect somebody who will try something different. In non-democratic countries, I believe that, while of course individuals are not free to vote, actually governments know that if they pursue deeply unpopular policies or face a crisis, then there will be a consequence in terms of popular support. The growth in the use of mobile telephones and the Internet has added enormous force to this phenomenon. While the uprisings of the 'Arab Spring' are yet to deliver economic prosperity, change is clearly afoot. Similarly, while the political elite of Beijing rule the country with a strong central purpose, their policies adapt and change according to what their Internet-using populace complain about. Indeed, there are signs that Chinese political leaders actively monitor and respond to discontent expressed online.

Given the rising political pressure in those countries experiencing little or no growth, it is becoming less and less fashionable to support the more simplistic aspects of the Reinhart and Rogoff thesis. Unless forced by financial market pressures, governments will probably have to be more flexible in trying to reduce their national debt burdens as a goal in itself.

Given the current mood in the United Kingdom and elsewhere, and given the economic challenges since 2009, it has become fashionable to look to the German model in view of their prowess as a manufacturing exporter. But while this is understandable, it is certainly not obvious to me that every other country should be rushing to mimic Germany's economic framework. It is simply not feasible for every country to follow the same model. Germany's success in recent years has essentially been a consequence of successfully exporting to meet the growing demand of the BRIC economies, especially Russia and China. If the Chinese economy were to experience a so-called hard landing, with many years of weak growth, then Germany would face considerable consequences. It might even change German thinking about appropriate policies for the struggling European countries, as Germany would find itself unable to export to weak neighbours to make up for any serious China shortfall. Some economists argue anyway that Germany should pursue more vigorously a policy aimed at driving up domestic demand to make it an engine of GDP growth, boosting German imports and helping to rebalance the eurozone by offering better export prospects to other members. In addition, while it is now fashionable to admire the German export and manufacturing machine, some of us recall the early 1990s when the phrase 'eurosclerosis' was widely used to describe the seeming inability of Germany to reform and attract investment.

Here in the United Kingdom, the mantra is that the structure of the British economy must be rebalanced away from financial services and towards manufacturing, and while some shift in this direction is probably appropriate, it is not a panacea, nor easy to engineer. The United Kingdom has its own advantages to offer the rest of the world, just as Germany and others do. Our time zone, the growing global use of our language, the rapid mass adoption of the Internet and mobile telephony, and the innovations surrounding them all suggest a big advantage for the United Kingdom in being a global services provider with finance remaining at its heart. The need for better and more effectively regulated financial services is one thing, but there is no clear need to reduce the financial sector. Neither should there be a question as to whether British banks did become too large for the health of the overall economy. There is a big difference between what British banks should be doing for the benefit of the domestic UK economy and what international banks – British and otherwise – should be encouraged to do from the United Kingdom in terms of the services they offer to the rest of the world. Trying to ensure that the domestic British banking system is

neither too big nor too small and that it is adequately capitalized is of course necessary, but taking strong views beyond
that is dangerous. Banks need different levels of capital during downturns compared with booms; this would be an obvious measure to implement. The City of London provides a
unique service to the world, one it would be difficult to match
elsewhere. Its accumulation of knowledge and specialist services provides the United Kingdom with a lasting and important competitive advantage. The City should be encouraged
to prosper, because more and more of its services will be de-
manded by a greater number of emerging economies as they
grow.

Despite this defence of the City, which some might read as
defending the status quo, I have considerable sympathy for
the notion of a government-owned bank, and certainly any
government wanting to alter the structure of its economy will
probably need to undertake some of the necessary financing
and investment directly.

Which brings me to China and its distinctive brand of capitalism. It is presumed by many that as China develops and individuals get wealthier they will become more and more like 'us'
in all aspects of their lives, including how their financial institutions behave as well as their individual political freedoms
and choices. This is ironic at a time when there are so many
complaints about how our banks are not lending enough to
business or consumers and that they should be made to do
more, regardless of their own perception of profitability. Another way of putting it is that, in some ways, we would like our
banks to be a bit more Chinese. Their big banks are still under
different degrees of state control and it is rare for any of
them to pursue policies that do not support the central goals
of economic policy, usually highlighted in great clarity in the
Five-Year Plan. It is not obvious that China will leave its model

permanently unchanged, especially given signs of strain in the banking sector, but it is interesting that some people in the United Kingdom and elsewhere have called for our system to be, in this respect, a little more like China's.

Another area where we in the United Kingdom and the West can stand to learn from some of the Growth Market economies is with respect to infrastructure spending. This might seem a little odd at first read, as amongst the biggest challenges facing many of the Growth Markets is an infrastructure one. But some, including South Korea and China, have successfully developed parts of their infrastructure to benefit their economies, and the other Growth Markets can learn from this – as, perhaps, can we. I talked about South Korea's strong scoring in terms of growth environment scores, which are helped by education and their technological prowess. To a more limited degree, some parts of China, notably Shanghai, seem to be advancing rapidly in terms of education, and, of course, there is much to be learned from Beijing and Shanghai airports in terms of infrastructure effects.

In the end, we should not be dogmatic about which model of capitalism is 'right'. Germany's prudent, export-oriented model looks somewhat attractive now compared with the buccaneering 'Anglo-Saxon' approach of the 2000s. But a decade earlier, Germany had seemed sclerotic. On the other hand, many in the West are sceptical about whether China's model can be sustained: will Chinese people not demand more freedoms as their level of income and education rises? Of course, the country faces some challenging social and political developments. Yet, as the central player in the world economy, China has some lessons the West could usefully apply, including reflecting on the role the state plays in the economy. We have an unusual opportunity to learn from the successes and failures of both other Western economies and the BRIC economies, and to select those aspects of policy that seem most relevant to our current circumstances. Adaptability will be the key to future economic growth.

The time for dogma is past. Both the 2008 Western crisis and the 15–20 years of BRIC growth have redrawn the map of the world economy. Adaptive capitalism is the right solution, with policymakers everywhere needing to become more flexible and open to lessons from elsewhere in this new world.

Endnotes

1. Jim O'Neill. 2013. *The Growth Map: Economic Opportunity in the BRICs and Beyond*. Portfolio Penguin.

2. John Plender. 2013. EM decoupling story was always over-hyped, FT.com, 14 August 2013.

3. Albert Edwards. 2011. Société Générale, Bloody ridiculous investment concept, 7 December 2011.

4. Jim O'Neill. 2011. Project Syndicate, 7 February 2011. Goldman Sachs Asset Management.

5. Dominic Wilson, Kamakshya Trivedi, Stacy Carlson and Jose Ursua. 2011. The BRICs 10 years on: halfway through the great transformation. Global Economics Paper 217, GS Global ECS Research, 7 December 2011.

6. Jim O'Neill, Dominic Wilson, Roopa Purushothaman and Anna Stupnytska. 2005. How solid are the BRICs? Global Economics Paper 134, GS Global ECS Research, 1 December 2005.

7. OECD PISA scores, 9 December 2010.

8. Xia Bin. 2013. Logic and roadmap of China's economic reform, *First Financial Newspaper*, 31 January 2013.

9. Human Development Report (UNDP). 2013. *The Rise of the South: Human Progress in a Diverse World*. United Nations Development Programme.

10. Mexico drives North American auto investment, challenges China. Reuters, 21 October 2013.

11. Growing pains: Africa's populations look set to soar by 2100. *The Economist*, 5 May 2011.

12. Jim O'Neill and Anna Stupnytska. 2010. How exciting is Africa's potential? Goldman Sachs Asset Management, Strategy Series, 14 October 2010.

13. Jim O'Neill. 2001. Building better global economic BRICs. Global Economics Paper 66, GS Global ECS Research, November 2001.

14. Jim O'Neill. 2003. Dreaming with BRICs: the path to 2050. Global Economics Paper 99, GS Global ECS Research, October 2003.

15. Jim O'Neill and Robert Hormats. 2004. The G8: time for a change. Global Economics Paper 112, GS Global ECS Research, 3 June 2004.

16. Kevin Daly. 2013. *GS European Economics Daily*, 22 May 2013.

17. Carmen M. Reinhart and Kenneth Rogoff. 2011. *This Time Is Different: Eight Centuries of Financial Folly.* Princeton University Press.

18. Carmen M. Reinhart and Kenneth Rogoff. 2010. Growth in the time of debt. *American Economic Review* 100:573–78.

19. Thomas Herndon, Michael Ash and Robert Pollin. 2013. Does high public debt consistently stifle economic growth? A critique of Reinhart and Rogoff. University of Massachusetts, 3 June 2013.